L.I.F.E. BIBLE COLLEGE EAST
LIBRARY
CHRISTIANSBURG, VA.

150812

S0-ATJ-652

Baby
Mayfield

Baby Mayfield

by

LARRY & DIANE MAYFIELD

WITH
JERRY B. JENKINS

MOODY PRESS

CHICAGO

© 1989 by
LARRY AND DIANE MAYFIELD and JERRY B. JENKINS

All rights reserved. No part of this book may be reproduced in any form without permission in writing from the publisher, except in the case of brief quotations embodied in critical articles or reviews.

All Scripture quotations, unless noted otherwise, are from *The Holy Bible, New International Version,* copyright © 1973, 1978, 1984 by the International Bible Society. Used by permission of Zondervan Bible Publishers.

ISBN: 0-8024-1116-9

1 2 3 4 5 6 Printing/LC/Year 93 92 91 90 89

Printed in the United States of America

241.69760922
M4536

LIFE Pacific College
Alumni Library
1100 West Covina Blvd.
San Dimas, CA 91773

*To the Christian friends
who joined us on our journey of faith,
praying, encouraging, ministering people of God
from Nashville and Brentwood, Tennessee,
Fremont, California, Hot Springs Village, Arkansas,
Zion, Illinois, and all over the country.*

*To our children, our parents,
Walter and Lois Mays and Willis and Edith Mayfield,
our extended families, and to Brenda and Gail,
for being there.*

*With special memories of
Bob Benson and Connie Birky Edwards,
who stood with us in prayer
despite their own physical struggles.
Both are now with the Lord.*

L.I.F.E. BIBLE COLLEGE EAST
LIBRARY
CHRISTIANSBURG, VA
05184

CONTENTS

ACKNOWLEDGMENTS

I gratefully acknowledge the generosity of the Mayfields in revealing their thoughts and emotions, for providing access to documents and records, and for reliving a painful year during endless hours of interviewing. Diane's written recollections were of particular value.

Names and insignificant details have been changed where appropriate to protect identities. Otherwise the story has been recreated as faithfully as possible from documents and the memories of those involved.

JERRY B. JENKINS

PREFACE

The idea for this book came from songwriter Ron Harris, a dear friend of the Mayfields, who insisted that they chronicle what God did in their lives during the difficult period covered in this book. He also wrote this song, dedicated to Larry and Diane:

Oh, So Much

Oh, so much. I love You, Lord, oh, so much.
I love You, Lord, oh so much that I will do anything You ask of me. I will do anything You ask of me. I will do anything You ask of me at all.
Oh, so much. I need You, Lord, oh, so much.
I need You, Lord, oh so much. And I will do anything You ask of me. I will do anything You ask of me. I will do anything You ask of me at all.
Oh, so much. I'll praise You, Lord, oh so much.
I'll praise You, Lord, oh so much. And I will do anything you ask of me. I will do anything You ask of me. I will do anything You ask of me at all.

© Copyright 1988 by Ron Harris Music. All rights reserved. International copyright secured. Used by permission.

11

INTRODUCTION
A New Thing

Behold, I will do a new thing,
Now it shall spring forth;
Shall you not know it?
I will even make a road in the wilderness
And rivers in the desert.
(Isaiah 43:19, NKJV*)

Larry and Diane Mayfield always take a Bible verse as their New Year's resolution. When God gave them Isaiah 43:19 for 1985, with its promise of "a new thing," Diane thought she knew what it meant. She thought it related to several exciting projects on which she and Larry were working. Surely this would be the year when the vagaries of self-employment would end. Something would hit that would make life easier, or at least more predictable.

God had been doing "new things" for Diane Mayfield for two decades. The pretty blonde was in her late thirties, married to a free-lance composer, arranger, and producer who had become a mainstay in Christian music during the past twenty years.

* *New King James Version.*

13

Theirs had been a storybook romance. Diane remembers seeing Larry as a teenager when his family, "The Musical Mayfields," performed at her church. Larry played both trombone and piano. Later he had been three years ahead of her at Moody Bible Institute in Chicago, and his reputation as a prodigy had preceded him. (He had begun college at sixteen.) They met on an elevator in the music building, and it was love at first sight. Both were musical, intelligent, friendly, and well brought up. Each recognized the potential for a serious relationship from the beginning and carefully nurtured their future.

They had married in 1967, the day after Diane graduated, and in the ensuing seventeen and a half years had enjoyed an unusually strong and healthy marriage. They had been through a lot together and were pleased to have come to this season of life liking each other as much as they loved each other.

Both are creative and, Larry admits, "volatile, so sometimes sparks fly. But for us, that's good. We speak our minds. Things are out in the open. We're both able to apologize and to accept apologies. With a few minor bumps and bruises along the way, we've had a good marriage."

For them divorce is not an option; God's grace has allowed them to work through diversity together. Diane says that the only time she locked herself in the bathroom was "to get away from the kids!"

The kids began arriving in the Mayfields' lives on November 22, 1970, when they adopted Tracie, a three-day-old, blue-eyed blonde. After having struggled through the pain of learning that they would not be able to have their own children, they were eager to adopt. Ahead of the abortion epidemic by three years, they had little trouble effecting a private adoption, which was hardly the case three and a half years later when they hoped to adopt again.

Diane recalls being all but laughed from the room when she and Larry expressed their desire at an agency. "It

14

was too difficult, next to impossible. Plus they wanted several thousand dollars."

"We were virtually told, 'Forget it,' " Larry recalls. "We were made to feel stupid and naive for even thinking we could adopt another baby. We left with our heads spinning, thrilled that we had gotten Tracie when we did. If we could have only one child, that would be just fine."

The Mayfields didn't even pray that they would have any more children, but they didn't know that others were praying that they would. Not long after that discouraging trip to the adoption agency, Diane came home from the doctor with news for Larry. "I'm pregnant."

"Nah," he said. "Can't be! Call 'em back and make sure." She did. They were sure.

When Diane told Tracie of the baby God had placed inside her, Tracie said, "Just like I was inside of you."

"Well, you were inside me in a different way," Diane said, having already told Tracie they had chosen her. "You were in my heart before we ever saw you."

When Jeffrey was born June 9, 1975, they called him "our miracle boy." The Mayfields considered Jeff a once-in-a-lifetime bonus who gave them the perfect family: a girl and a boy.

The following year, the "new thing" in the Mayfields lives was tragedy. Diane's older brother Brian had been an outstanding high school athlete and had gone on to become a successful civil engineer. Diane loved him and idolized him, and he was particularly close to Tracie. Diane had worried about his health for years, though, for he had suffered from colitis since high school.

Larry and Diane had just visited Brian and his bride of a year when they heard that he was going to the hospital for tests. That was nothing unusual for Brian in light of his medical history, and they remarked that he had not looked well during their recent visit with him. He had hidden his health problems for years, but now he looked really sick.

Diane and Larry assumed his troubles with colitis had flared up again.

But the news from Brian's doctors in Chicago was much worse. Brian had developed abdominal cancer so advanced it was inoperable. Given two months to live, he was dead within two weeks.

"He was my hero," Diane says. "It was hard to be without him. It was very hard on Tracie, too. Our only consolation was that our separation from Brian would not last forever."

The following year, 1977, Larry followed the recording and music publishing business to Nashville, and he and Diane found a house with a bedroom for each child.

It was a major move, and though the house was modest by Brentwood, Tennessee, standards, it was more than they had ever expected to own. Both Larry and Diane fought the materialism that threatened to creep into their professional and private lives. Larry gravitated toward the people in the Christian music industry who didn't play games, and Diane worked with him to instill spiritual values in their children.

The Mayfields had been in Tennessee less than a year when Diane became pregnant again. Though they thought their family was complete and perfect, both Larry and Diane were overjoyed at the thought of another baby. "After having been told we couldn't have children," Larry says, "we felt especially blessed."

The doctor was an Alabama alumnus who promised to personally deliver the baby unless it came the day of the Alabama-Auburn football game. "Fortunately," Larry says, "Shelley was born October 12, 1978, which was midweek. The doctor handed me the baby and said, 'Don't fumble.' "

This second daughter was another "new thing" in their lives from the Lord, and the Mayfields settled into a life of hectic work and homemaking, Diane still trying to help Larry when she could, despite the demands of three children. She wasn't conscious of feeling the pressure to be Super Mom, but that's how she might have been described. She was active in church, in school, car-pooling, and in Larry's work.

More than anything, she wanted her home to be a place of refuge, of spiritual strength, a place where her children would develop character and biblical values. Her family became one of traditions, of New Year's resolutions and New Year's verses, of Christmas tree ornaments for each child each year.

For Christmas 1980 there were four children's ornaments. Diane was pregnant again, and happy about it. Though it had been a surprise, even a shock, to be pregnant again, she was soon excited and eager to be a mother once more.

But the pregnancy was difficult. By the third month she felt large, and uncomfortable, and sick. When the doctor informed Diane that the baby had died within her, she and Larry were grief-stricken. One day not long afterwards, a neighbor who had heard the news rushed to Larry in tears, telling him how sorry she was. He realized he felt the same way and finally understood how difficult miscarriages can be. "Some people think it's easier than losing a born child," he says, "but it was awful. It was sad."

Larry and Diane wept together in the hospital while they waited. Then Diane was taken to the obstetrics ward, where the air buzzed with the happy conversation of couples talking about impending births or hours-old babies. In a labor room, Diane was struck with the fact that the procedures were the same as they had been for Shelley's birth, but this time the outcome would be different. There would be no happy ending.

Though there would be no baby, there was a mother, washed through with the hormone flood that accompanies pregnancy and delivery. There was the motherly instinct and love, the need to hold the new baby. Diane was grate-

17

ful to be moved to another floor when the operation was over, and she grieved.

Larry grieved too, but in Diane's mind, he got over it more quickly. She wanted to replace her loss, to try for another child. But by the end of the summer she had begun to recover. Still, it took her longer than normal to shed the extra pounds, and though in her mind she had accepted the miscarriage, her body and her emotions ached.

"I felt such a void," she says. Yet she found that time was her friend. There was no long period of bitterness or anger. She was all the more thankful for the three children she had. Larry was pleased when he noticed that Diane was getting back in the swing of her typical schedule.

"Diane has always been a very on-the-go, strong, driving personality," he says, "up tempo with lots of endurance. She was active as all get out and loved being busy. It was good to see her back on top."

Besides all her other activities, Diane helped Larry write a patriotic musical, "Kids for America," which they directed and performed locally and then saw succeed as a publishing venture. Such efforts are grueling but satisfying, so if Diane began to notice fatigue or muscle strain or back pain, she thought it was related to all the activity, to her age, or to her three pregnancies.

By the summer of 1984, Tracie had become a delightful teenager, Jeff was nine, and Shelley was pushing six. Diane spent much of her spare time on the floor poring over pictures and memories as she put together a book of Larry's life for his fortieth birthday. It was at the neighborhood pool that she first became aware that her back was bothering her. What had begun as a niggling feeling of pressure in her lower back now became pain strong enough to make it impossible for her to sit in the lounge chairs.

Diane mentioned her discomfort to friends, and they passed along advice their chiropractors and neurologists had given them about similar maladies. She knew it was mostly secondhand information with some old wives' tales thrown in, but she thought that was better than the expense of going for treatment and advice on her own.

When Shelley started kindergarten, Diane and the other parents had to fill in until a teacher could be hired. They built a playhouse for the children, painting and crawling beneath construction projects. Diane was uncomfortable and finally in real pain, but she reasoned that Larry was helping out too, in spite of his schedule and his chronically bad knees (even after arthroscopic surgery he was in constant pain in both knees), so she "just kept at it."

By fall she had dropped out of Bible Study Fellowship because she could no longer sit through the sessions. The pressure on her lower back was bad, "like a constant weight. I could tell it wasn't a muscle spasm. I knew it was more of a disk problem." When she drove, Diane often felt a sudden jolt of pain starting at her back and running all the way down her right leg, pain so sharp she screamed. Then it would leave as quickly as it came.

By the end of the year Diane and Larry were involved in the staging, costumes, choreography—and all the rest —of an ambitious Christmas musical play. Diane found the work so stimulating and so much fun she doesn't remember her back bothering her at all during the run of the play.

As in the past, as the calendar edged toward Christmas, she felt a certain pressure to make family life something special. "I invested all my energies, physically and emotionally, into the holidays." And she and Larry had many reasons to look ahead to the new year with great optimism. They were deeply involved in an animated musical that appeared to be headed for a television series. It was the type of work and the type of break that free lancers dream of. Besides being wholesome and destined to compete with most vapid children's television, it could lead to steady, creative work in Larry's specialty.

That's why, when the Mayfields felt led to Isaiah 43:19 for their 1985 New Year's verse, Diane was sure she knew what "new thing" God was promising. Had she known how wrong she was, had she known how soon she would find out how wrong she was, or had she known what she would have to endure before learning what God wanted to teach her, she might have wished 1985 would never come.

1

Happy New Year

Diane Mayfield's back was not getting better. At times the pain extended into her leg and made it almost impossible to get in and out of the car. She had been to a chiropractor only for headaches, and she had never been treated for what now caused her the most discomfort.

She couldn't know that one of her vertebral discs—flat, coin-shaped rings of cartilage that surround a soft, pulpy center and serve as shock absorbers between the bones in her spinal column—was beginning to rupture, to slip out of position.

She couldn't have told you then that the disc in question was between the fourth and fifth lumbar region vertebrae, or that the soft center had begun to squeeze out through a weak point in the encircling cartilage and press on a nearby spinal nerve. All she knew was that it hurt.

By the middle of February Diane had decided to see Larry's orthopedic doctor. On February 19 he X-rayed her back and informed her she had "degenerative disc disease. I can prescribe muscle relaxants to make it less painful, but I'm afraid it's a fact of life at your age and that you should expect to experience discomfort from this point on."

The muscle relaxants had little, if any, effect. Soon the pain kept her awake at night. Eventually the orthopedist seemed to change his opinion. Maybe it wasn't the disc. Diane felt free to let her chiropractor try to adjust her spine. He also took an X ray, then manipulated her spine. It still hurt, but some pressure was relieved and made it possible for her to drive. And to sleep occasionally.

At the end of the month the chiropractor fitted her with a brace to keep her spine in place. Diane hoped it would be the answer. She still tried denying even to herself that she had a serious problem. Pressure was building in her back, but if she could learn to use the brace properly, she could function. She had places to go, things to do.

There was the big fund raising banquet coming up the first week of March, and shortly after that the Mayfields had planned a family getaway to Gatlinburg, a four-hour drive to the Smokey Mountains. In her continuing quest to protect her children from worldly values and to infuse them with Christian principles, Diane had prepared spiritual notebooks for each. This would be no mere vacation, she decided. The family was going to grow spiritually.

The only problem was that even a night out at a nice banquet was an ordeal for Diane. Still trying to keep from admitting even to herself that her problem was serious, she might complain to Larry about pain in her leg but not tell him that she needed help in getting stockings and shoes on. Tracie might have to help her with her panty hose, and Diane had to go through contortions just to get her shoes on.

Then, at the dinner, she walked as if in slow motion, agonizingly lifting her leg. When the other women congregated in the rest rooms between the meal and the program, she stayed where she was. She felt guilty concentrating so much on her pain when her pastor's wife sat at the same table with excruciating TMJ, the result of an auto accident years before. *If she can persevere, so can I,* Diane told herself.

Judy Parrish, a friend who once worked for a group of neurosurgeons, noticed Diane seemed in pain at the banquet. "How are you doing?" she asked.

"Oh, not too well. A little stiff."

Judy had known of Diane's minor lower back pain, but this was clearly out of the ordinary. "You should see a doctor," she said. "Get an appointment with a neurosurgeon."

"Oh, well, maybe," Diane said, plainly politely passing off the suggestion.

Later Judy pulled Larry off to the side. "What's wrong with Diane?" she asked.

"She's got some pain in her leg, I guess," he said.

"It's worse than that, Larry. Look at her. Watch her walk. This is more than a backache or leg pain. I think something's really wrong."

Larry appreciated Judy's concern and began to be more aware of Diane's discomfort, but that only made her more determined to carry on. She did not want to slow down, to be an invalid, or, especially, to be treated like one. She wanted to do and be everything she could for her family, and needing her husband to help dress her would be to admit she was caving in to pain. It would pass. It had to pass.

After the four-hour drive to Gatlinburg the next week, it was time to walk around and visit the shops. The hilly area was the worst thing for a spine that had been in a sitting position. The pain affected Diane's mood, and, she confesses, "I was acting horrible to everybody. The pain was just killing me, but I wouldn't admit it."

"None of us knew what was wrong with Diane," Larry says. "The kids and I couldn't figure her out."

But even she didn't know that it was the pain, the all-consuming pain, that made her the woman she was during those few days. She was a relentless taskmaster, insisting that the kids work faster on their spiritual notebooks. When they wanted to be out playing and seeing the sights, she got on them them for being too slow in looking up verses, in finishing artwork, in growing spiritually. "This is a spiritual retreat," she reminded them more than once. "I was terrible," she says now.

Diane grew more nervous, more irritated that the kids didn't seem to care about their spiritual notebooks. When they did take breaks, she slipped into the shower and tried to massage her back with hot water, still trying to convince herself that this was something that would take care of itself.

She forced herself to go shopping with Tracie, to ignore the pain in her back and the frightening numbness in her leg. It was important to gather the spiritual mementos that would make this trip the rich memory she intended it to be. She wanted to go through the woods to the off beat places in Gatlinburg, away from the crowds and commercialism. Larry had to stop occasionally so Diane could adjust the Velcro straps on her back brace. "Oh, Mom!" the kids would complain. "Please don't do that in public." Diane was near desperation, still not admitting anything, still insisting on going forward. It wasn't as if she had a choice. She certainly wouldn't struggle painfully out of the car and tug at brace straps if she didn't have to.

The trip was becoming a failure, she knew, and that just made her more miserable. When they returned home, she was woeful. She told her chiropractor, "You have to do something, because the brace just doesn't work." She complained of the numbness in her leg. He pulled it hard, and though it was still numb, the manipulation relieved some of the pressure that "kept building, building like a ton of pressure in my back."

When she was able to hobble back to her car and drive home, she sighed. "I made it!" She had seen people limp into chiropractor's offices and walk out a little better. "I figured that was what life was going to be for me."

24

One of the things Diane feels God was dealing with her about during this time was her compulsion to be perfect for her family. "My husband was known in the music community, but we both made it a point not to let that pressure me into playing a certain role. We had dealt with that temptation before we moved to Nashville. Yet, in my mind, I wanted to be the perfect mother and keep working with Larry in what he was creating. We were our closest when we created together. Meanwhile, I had the conviction that I wanted our family to be different, to not be so commercial or materialistic or acquisitive. I reasoned that our parents on both sides were too far away, and we were too far from cousins and other support groups. When you get it in your mind that there just isn't anyone else around who cares as much as you do, you're in a trap, but that's where I was. I not only had to be a spiritual model to my family, despite all the other pressures I brought on myself, but I had to be my own support system too." There was no one else. At least that was her thinking at the time. She had to be Super Woman. She didn't have time for pain, for discomfort, for incapacity.

In mid-March it was fun to have fourteen-year-old Tracie home from school on spring break, even though Jeff (nine) and Shelley (six) still had to be readied for school each day. Larry was in his pajamas, shaving, and Tracie was sleeping in as Diane knelt on the floor in the living room, helping Shelley with her clothes. Jeff was ready and waiting by the door for the bus that would pick them up right out front.

Diane heard and felt something snap in her lower back, unaware that a huge chunk of the soft center of the disc between her fourth and fifth lumbar vertebrae had smashed through the cartilage ring and speared its way into the spinal nerve. She screamed out in pain, and Shelley's eyes grew huge.

Diane struggled to her feet as Jeff and Shelley looked on in horror. From the bathroom Larry heard, "Help me! Help me! Oh, help me!" He ran to the living room. "You've got to help me!"

"What is it?"

"I don't know! My back! Help! Please! Do something!"

He helped her into the bathroom and drew hot water into the tub. She moved gingerly as she continued to scream, trying to find a position somewhere, anywhere that would take the awful pain away. It was as if the pain itself were alive, with a mind and a personality all its own. It ravaged her, wounded her, stabbed her, and there was no letup.

Somehow Larry got her undressed and into the tub, but it didn't work, nothing worked. It was worse! She screamed and screamed, "Help me! Help me!" Jeff and Shelley listened from the door. "You've got to do something! You've got to help me!"

Larry hurried to the living room and ushered Jeff and Shelley outside. "Everything's going to be all right, kids. We'll take care of Mommy. By the time you get home, she'll be fine."

They said nothing, not a word, terror etched in their faces. Larry wanted them out of the house so they wouldn't have to experience any more of their mother's screaming. He hadn't believed a word he had said about her being all right, but he didn't know what else to say. Get them out, away from this, was all he could think to do.

Back in the bathroom Diane writhed in pain, still screaming, "Help me! Somebody help me!"

Larry was frustrated, panicky himself. He would have done anything he knew to do, but he knew nothing. This pain, this back problem, this leg numbness had erupted into a nightmare of agony. He loved his wife enough to want to take the pain from her, to make it his own. If whatever had happened was going to kill someone with agony, let it be him. But what could he do?

26

As he lifted her from the tub, her shrieks echoing deafeningly off the tile walls, she quit screaming, but only for an instant. What had he done? Had there been something in the way he held her, moved her, carried her that offered some tiny bit of relief?

He had bent over the tub. She had slowly reached up and clasped her hands behind his neck. When he had straightened up, he had lifted her. She had raised her legs to clear the edge of the tub. And there, hanging from his neck, her feet off the ground, her weight had caused the vertebrae to pull apart just enough to take some of the pressure off the disc so it didn't push so hard against the piece that had broken off and embedded itself into the nerve.

Neither knew why this position offered any relief, but both knew that any other position—standing, sitting, leaning, lying—simply didn't work. Despite more wailing and screaming, Larry moved her enough to put on her sweat suit. "If she could have moved, she'd have beat me up, because even dressing her like a baby made the pain unbearable." Moving out of the bathroom and to the bedroom made Diane scream out again and again, filling the house with that unnatural sound, waking Tracie and bringing her running.

She found her mother hanging from her father's neck in the bedroom, crying from the pain, screaming whenever Larry shifted his weight to keep from cramping up himself. Diane was at the point of desperation. Death would have been a relief, the suffering was so intense.

Larry wanted to ask her what she thought he should do, what did she want him to do, should he get dressed, get her dressed, what? "What can I do?" was all that would come out. He was answered with screams. "Help me! Help me! Do something! Larry! What are we going to do?"

"I don't know what to do!" he said. "We have to get help!"

Tracie took over holding Diane while Larry rested his aching, quivering knees and pressed his back against the wall. When he took her back from Tracie, she cried out again. "Get my phone book, Tracie! Let's call the doctor."

This, they all knew, was far beyond the scope of a chiropractor. Tracie dialed the orthopedist, and Larry held the receiver to Diane's ear as it rang. "Doctor's office," a voice said.

"I need to talk to him right away."

"I'm sorry. He's away on spring vacation and the office is closed."

2
A Ride to Forget

The next hour was nightmarish. Hanging from Larry's neck, her feet off the ground, was the only position that relieved pressure from the disc fragment that had embedded itself in Diane's spinal nerve. Still, no one knew what caused such excruciating pain. Diane screamed and cried with every tiny move. Larry had never seen her like this, not in their entire life together.

He worried he would do something that would make things worse, that she would be paralyzed. Visions invaded his mind of her in a wheelchair the rest of her life. His back knotted with cramps, his legs wavered. He backed up against the wall, trying to stay straight and not move while bearing his precious load.

"Maybe I should try to get you to the emergency room," he said.

Diane whimpered. "But which one? And what doctor? I can't move!"

Switching Diane to Tracie's neck was an ordeal. The screaming, the agony, the weeping made the minutes drag by. Tracie was enough shorter than Larry that Diane's knees now brushed the ground. Tracie, with her natural sense of humor, tried to lighten the scene. "What did you do over spring break?" she deadpanned. "Oh, while everyone else was in the Bahamas, I went with my family to Gatlinburg, and my mother hung around my neck the rest of the time."

She laughed nervously. Even Diane smiled, but she dared not laugh. Laughing meant moving, and moving meant pain. She couldn't imagine any relief other than death, and though she didn't say it, more than anything in the world she wanted to die. Quickly. Quietly. Painlessly. Please.

Her wrists ached from supporting herself. When Larry or Tracie tried to reach up and hold her arms so she wouldn't have the entire burden, it threw them off balance or moved Diane too much. And the screaming began again.

"Lord, please tell us what to do!"

Diane believes God put the thought in her mind to call Judy Parrish. *Judy used to work for neurosurgeons,* she thought, *and I've asked her advice before. She was concerned about me at the banquet the other night. But she's rarely at home. She could be taking her kids to school or be out for breakfast, anything.*

"Give me the phone," Diane managed. Her face was locked in a grimace of torment as she hoped and prayed that Judy would answer. She did.

Diane was nearly delirious from the pain but the information gushed from her. "Judy, something's happened to my back, I don't know what. I'm hanging from Larry's neck right now. I need a doctor. What can I do?"

Judy didn't hesitate or ask questions. She could tell from Diane's voice that this was a real emergency. "I'll call Dr. Bradford,"* she said. "I'll call you right back."

The wait seemed eternal. Diane knew Dr. Bradford was a highly regarded specialist with a practice closed to new patients, other than referrals from other doctors. She

* Not his real name.

imagined his taking a call from a former employee and begging off or suggesting somewhere else for Diane to be taken. The pain threatened to kill her, and she wished it would.

The phone rang. Tracie held it to her mother's ear. "Yes?"

"Dr. Bradford is in surgery at Memorial. He says if you can get to the emergency room there, he'll see you as soon as the operation is finished."

Memorial? That was forty-five minutes away on the north side of Nashville. Diane knew she had no choice. She thanked Judy, told Larry, and nearly passed out when he shifted her to Tracie so he could get dressed. He brought her two pain pills from the prescription he used for his knees. Diane is the type who avoids even aspirin as a rule, but she downed these eagerly. They would have no effect on the pain, but she was willing to try anything.

As soon as Larry was ready, Diane was transferred back to his neck while Tracie hurriedly packed a bag for her. Diane was amazed that any pain could be so intense, so sharp, so long-lasting. Past the minuscule lessening of the pressure when she was suspended from Larry's or Tracie's neck, nothing stanched the shooting, throbbing, piercing torture. She dreaded even the thought of getting from the bedroom to the garage. It was a infernal trek.

Facing Larry, her head on his shoulder, her hands clasped behind his neck, her feet raised behind her, Diane screamed over and over, "Oh, no! Help me! I can't do this! Larry, stop, I can't make it! Help me! Help me! Help me!" He edged out of the bedroom, taking slow, short steps, hardly lifting his feet, trying to keep from moving her from right to left, trying not to bounce. He knew he had to get her into the car, but he didn't even want to think about how. He had to get her out of the bedroom, down the hall, through the family room, through the kitchen, out the door to the garage, down two concrete steps, around the Mus-

31

tang, and into the passenger's side of the station wagon. Walking coast to coast seemed quicker.

Though her mind was fuzzy from the pills, the pain was worse. Her thoughts were jumbled, overridden by such agony that all she could do, all the way down the hall, was plead for help. Regardless of what Larry did, it wasn't enough. Neither dared think whether she had permanently damaged her spine, broken her back, torn a muscle, shattered a bone. Larry wanted to help Diane. Diane wanted to die.

Tracie ran ahead, opening doors, clearing the path, while Larry instructed her to stay home during the day, to be there when her brother and sister got home, to fix dinner. He would call. Her vacation was falling apart, but she wasn't complaining. She would do whatever was necessary to help her mother, to end this nightmare.

Larry is tall, strong, and wiry, not beefy. By now he had been holding Diane for the better part of an hour and for the last ten minutes carrying her deliberately through the house. The two steps down into the garage looked like a canyon. He couldn't rest, couldn't stop to scope it out. He wasn't sure, but time seemed of the essence. He hadn't considered whether this injury—whatever it was—was life-threatening. He just knew he wouldn't ask anyone to long endure such tribulation.

Diane swung sideways as he maneuvered through the door. She shrieked. He gingerly moved down first one step, waited, then the other. She wailed. He wanted to hurry around the smaller car, but he fought the urge in spite of rebelling muscles. Tracie opened the passenger side door and Larry backed in, Diane still hanging from his neck. Screaming.

There was no way to do that without moving and jostling and bumping Diane, but there was no other way to get her into the car. Larry slid across the seat to behind the wheel while Diane let her legs and lower torso slide off the seat. As Larry started the car, she still hung from his neck, most of her body off the seat. It had taken nearly fifteen minutes to get from the back bedroom to the car.

The drive to the hospital should have taken about forty-five minutes, had Larry known exactly how to get there and driven the speed limit. In spite of his haze over the precise directions, he would make it in thirty-five minutes, Diane passing out by the time he reached the intersection on Franklin Road and Old Hickory Boulevard, four miles away. She had fought and fought and fought the pain, and her mind and body could take no more. The light was red, and she could see the anxiety etched in Larry's face as he silently pleaded for the light to change. Unconsciousness was a relief, and she wouldn't come to until Larry wheeled into the emergency room driveway. He pushed it all the way up Route 65, hoping a policeman would notice and pull alongside. "I would have told him to lead me to Memorial fast."

Larry was thankful that Diane was out. "For two reasons," he admits. "First, it gave me a break from the screaming. Second, it gave me a break from the pressure of what I was supposed to do. I felt bad because I didn't know what to do. In fact, I felt like a complete, bumbling idiot. All I wanted to do was to help my bride, my love. But what was I supposed to do? With her unconscious and quiet, all I had to do was get her to the hospital. We were still in trouble, and I was still frightened, but for a little while I could focus on one task."

Larry prayed aloud, "Lord, you promised to go before us. Help me to trust You." Twenty minutes later, he parked in front of the door and carefully loosened Diane's grip on his neck. She didn't stir as he gently laid her head on the seat. He went in for help in getting Diane out of the car and was informed of hospital policy. He had to get her out of the car himself, and she had to enter the hospital in a wheelchair or on a gurney. Once she was in a chair or on a stretcher she became the responsibility of the hospital, but

L.I.F.E. BIBLE COLLEGE EAST
LIBRARY
CHRISTIANSBURG, VA.

not before. Larry knew he would have to carry her in himself anyway.

Larry leaned in from the driver's side and put Diane's arms up around his neck. She stirred and moaned, but as he straightened up and backed out, she was pulled across the seat and into the only position that had given her any relief since the injury occurred. As Larry slowly worked his way around the car and up the walk, a nurse's assistant wheeled a gurney out the door and down to the car. "Your wife has to come into the hospital on this," she said.

"That's all right," Larry said. "I've got her."

"No, I'm sorry, but she can't come in except on the bed."

"Well, she can't get on the bed. She's in intense pain," which should have been obvious from Diane's resumed screaming—and apologizing. Always aware of proper behavior and manners, it embarrassed her to be crying out. So as Larry carried her into the hospital, she would scream and apologize, scream and apologize.

"This isn't really how I am," she kept saying. "Really this isn't me." And she would scream again. "Oh, help me! I can't get on that bed!"

"Well," the woman said, "she has to. She's not coming in hanging around your neck."

"She has to," Larry insisted. "It's the only relief she gets from the pain."

"I'm sorry!" Diane said.

"I'm sorry," the woman said, now joined by two nurses. "We have to get you onto the bed."

"I can't! I can't! Please!"

"She can't!" Larry said. "Just let me get her in there, and we can talk about it."

"Sir, she is not going through that door except on the bed."

34

Diane pleaded and Larry tried to insist, but eventually they had to give in. Larry draped her sideways over the gurney so that she had one leg bent and the other hanging off the side, while she still hung from his neck. They were a sight working their way up the walk and through the door. Diane was still in misery, half on and half off the gurney, desperately clutching Larry, screaming and apologizing.

They were directed to the elevator and deposited on the third floor where they were to wait for Dr. Bradford. As soon as the doors opened, Larry lifted Diane off the bed to carry her to the examining room. Once again he was faced with hospital policy. A floor supervisor came running. "You can't carry her in here," she said. "She has to be in a wheelchair or on a bed."

Larry Mayfield is a man known to be direct, to speak his mind, sometimes even to vent his anger without raising his voice. He did not raise his voice this time either, but he was very direct and as serious as he could be. "Ma'am," he said, "I've heard that too many times already, and I don't want to hear it again. I'm going to be carrying her wherever she needs to go. She is in severe pain, and we don't know why. I am not going to subject her to a chair or a stretcher."

"But we can't allow—"

"Listen to me. I will carry her wherever you want us to wait for Dr. Bradford."

"Can you bring her in here?"

Larry followed the woman and other staff into a room where they were again required to put her on a bed. If possible, Diane's pain and desperation were worse than ever. She hung from Larry's neck, screaming, "I can't! I can't!" With everyone helping, and making every move in slow motion, they spent several agonizing minutes getting Diane face down in a hospital bed. She lay on her stomach with her legs splayed, feeling awkward and embarrassed, screaming and apologizing anew. She pleaded for something for the pain.

"I'm sorry," she was told. "I don't work for Dr. Bradford. Only he can prescribe something for you." Larry and Diane wondered if everyone thought she was faking.

"This is not how I usually am! I'm sorry! Somebody please help me! Do something! Give me something! Anything!"

3
The Decision

Diane lay across the bed on her stomach, one leg dangling, the other drawn up, one arm down, the other bent. Here was a woman with pride in her good posture. She had an image. And now her preferences were death, unconsciousness, a painkiller, hanging from Larry's neck, anything but this. She felt as if she was bobbing in a sea of unfriendly faces. The only person in the room who even seemed sympathetic was Larry, and his face was drawn with worry, concern, pity, frustration. She knew beyond doubt that he would do *anything* to relieve her pain, but neither of them knew what would do it.

Finally, after twenty minutes of suffering to the point of delirium, Diane saw a friendly, efficient countenance in the form of a smiling young woman. She breezed in, introducing herself as Kathy, Dr. Bradford's assistant. From the call from Judy Parrish she remembered Larry and Diane's names. She came directly to the bed. "You must be Diane."

Diane didn't dare move enough to nod. "Yes," she managed.

"Doctor Bradford will be right in from surgery," Kathy said.

"Can you give me something for this?" Diane pleaded.

"You haven't been given anything for pain? Of course I can."

She asked what had happened and how it had happened as she prepared an injection of morphine. Of course neither Larry nor Diane could shed any light on the situation, except for the brief history of Diane's back pain and the "something" that snapped that morning.

Kathy administered the shot in Diane's hip, and almost immediately a warm wave of relief washed over her. No amount of morphine, short of a dose that would have knocked Diane out, would have had a significant impact on a spinal nerve embedded with a huge chunk of disc, but the pain was dulled enough that Diane could move. She was still in an embarrassingly awkward position when Dr. Bradford arrived, but at least, at last, she could think. She could understand what people said. She could formulate answers that weren't clouded by blinding agony and her despairing of life.

Diane became aware that there was another patient in the room, and Diane felt sorry that she had been crying out while the woman was on the phone. "My head hurts so bad!" the woman had been telling a loved one. "The myelogram! Oh, my head!" The woman had stopped talking when Diane cried out, and Diane felt terrible that she was bothering her.

Dr. Bradford hurried in, pleasant, kind, smiling, but all business. He heard an immediate rundown of the case from Kathy, made sure the proper dose of morphine had been administered, spoke encouragingly to Diane, and then tested to see if she could move her toes. She could not. "I didn't know enough to even realize how serious that was," she recalls.

"I'm going to need to see a myelogram before I can determine a diagnosis," Dr. Bradford said.

Diane's heart sank. A myelogram? Wasn't that the one thing you never wanted to experience? That was what had given the woman in the next bed such a headache. But she knew there was no choice. She had to have it. The only improvement in her condition had been due to morphine that allowed her to move slightly and stop screaming. She knew she was still in deep, deep trouble, even if she didn't know why.

Larry asked that Diane be moved to a private room, and she was able to be rolled down the hall on her bed. "That was progress," Diane says, but she dreaded the wheelchair ride to the myelogram.

The doctor drew Larry aside and told him he was guessing that a disc had slipped and was pressing on a spinal nerve. "With this amount of pain and immobility, a portion of the disc may have broken loose and is putting pressure on the nerve. The myelogram will tell us one of three things. It could be that this is something we can treat with prescription medicines. It could be that surgery will be indicated, and we can keep her medicated, send her home, and decide when to do the operation. Or, we may find that immediate surgery is necessary, which we would probably do tomorrow."

"I was a naive layman," Larry says, "but I knew this was more serious than something that could be treated with medicine. I also seriously doubted we could take her home for a few days or weeks and schedule surgery later. Based on what had happened at home and by how much she had suffered, I was predicting option number three, and I would have been stunned to learn otherwise."

Besides your family, Diane always said, the two people you want and need most during a time of physical crisis are your doctor and your pastor. That's why she was so pleased and grateful to see her pastor, Millard Reed, standing in the doorway even before she went in for the myelogram. *How did he know I was here?* "Thankfully I was still in my jogging suit," she says. "I hadn't yet been issued a hospital gown."

Pastor Reed didn't stay long, but Diane appreciated that he personally made hospital calls and was just what she needed. "The Lord knew I needed him. He said, 'We're here for you. We want to do whatever we can.' "

"She'll probably have surgery," Larry told him before Pastor Reed left.

Larry wanted to go with Diane for the myelogram, but he was not permitted. He kissed her and told her he loved her, and she was wheeled away. He sat in her room, exhausted. And hungry. He had not realized until then that he had skipped breakfast. *But how can I go and get a sandwich while my wife is suffering?*

He decided she would want him to. In fact, she says, "I was so out of it by then, I didn't care what he did. Of course, he was better off getting food into his system than not, so it certainly didn't bother me to find out he had had a little lunch while I was having my test."

But it bothered Larry. He sat in the cafeteria thinking how good the food tasted when you were this hungry, but wondering what kind of a husband enjoys a meal at a time like that.

Larry was back in Diane's room when she returned from the myelogram. "The technician was very nice," she told him, her words slurred from fatigue and the effects of the morphine, which she was being given regularly now. "They did it in the lower back and he kept my head elevated, so I shouldn't have headaches or other side effects. He was really nice." She was blinking slowly and nearly nodded off. "It sure took a long time though."

Larry looked at his watch. "Over an hour," he said.

Diane nodded slightly and fell asleep. Larry was grateful. It was the first time he had seen her at peace since she passed out in the car. And that time she didn't appear too peaceful. That unconsciousness had been a result of pain, not of medication, and her face had been knotted in misery.

He knew she was still ailing, but she appeared to be sleeping soundly now.

Diane breathed deeply and was able to move to a more comfortable position. There was still pressure on her back, and nothing could take away that deep, dull pain, but before she drifted off completely she remembered the cold X-ray table where she was manipulated and maneuvered and put into position so the spinal fluid could be tapped and studied under the radiation. She also remembered that little sign near the X-ray machine: "Are you pregnant?"

That was a laugh. With all her pain and discomfort, she and Larry had not been able to make love more than once in the last two months. Of course, it only takes once, but that was a long shot. In fact, it wasn't even on her mind. Pregnancy was a non-issue. The Mayfields were not supposed to be able to have children anyway, so besides rhythm, they had never even worried about birth control.

Despite the fact that Diane finally seemed to be asleep, and Larry knew that was good for her, her sleep was fitful. Deep pain is an irritant to the sleeper, and she tossed and turned as much as her pain would allow. Larry tried to read and even to score some music. He thought of the responsibilities that lay ahead of him, even that night. He would have to check in with Tracie again and then get home and get some household chores and shopping done.

Dr. Bradford knocked gently. Larry rose; Diane didn't stir. "Don't get up," Dr. Bradford told Larry. He sat on the edge of the bed and whispered. "I've never seen a fracture like hers," he said. "A large piece of the disc between the fourth and fifth lumbar vertebrae broke loose and appears to be embedded in the nerve. It's no wonder she was in such pain."

"Then we have no choice," Larry said quietly.

"None whatsoever. There's pressure on the nerve from what I can tell from the myelogram. If we don't relieve that soon, she could have permanent nerve damage, would likely be paralyzed in at least the one leg, and might also lose voluntary function of her bladder and other organs."

"When would you like to do it?" Larry asked.

"I'd like to perform what we call a lumbarlaminectomy no later than tomorrow morning. I'm scheduled solid except for a break then."

"And you recommend it."

"Without question."

"The thought of back surgery is terrifying," Larry admitted.

"I understand fully," the doctor said. "If there was an option, I'd tell you. Not surgically repairing this is something you wouldn't even want to think about."

"Book it," Larry said. "Let's do it."

Before Larry left for home that evening, Diane awoke. He told her the results of the tests, the recommendation of the doctor, and his own response. "If I'd been awake when the doctor was in there," Diane says, "I might have remembered all the horror stories I'd heard about back surgery and begged for time to think about it. Now I was relieved, in a way, to know that I really had no choice. The decision had been made, and it was the only decision that could have been made. I was grateful for any hope of relief."

By the time Larry got home, Tracie had met the kids when they arrived on the bus, fed them, entertained them, and got them ready for bed. They were very curious about Mommy. Larry told them the whole story, then he and the three of them knelt and prayed for her. "We'll have to pray all the more tomorrow morning when she's in surgery," Larry said. "Can I count on you for that?"

Larry had always been of help to Diane around the house, but now he got the full impact of her responsibilities. He went to the grocery store in the middle of the night and saw an hour pass quickly as he stocked up. When he got home he threw in a couple of loads of wash. In the ensuing

days, then months, then years, he would come to the conclusion that there could no longer be any delineation between men's and women's work. He would vacuum and
dust and even try his hand at cooking. "I'm not a good
cook, and I can't sew," he says, "but you wind up doing
what you have to do. It began to dawn on me, and I became ashamed that I hadn't recognized it before, but perhaps I had taken her for granted. I had always appreciated
Diane, and I don't think I ever would have been categorized
as a chauvinist, but I sure learned that it's the rare husband
who works as hard as a housewife and mother. Their's is
thankless, endless work, and it's demanding and hard."

At that point the Mayfields had no idea how long
Diane would be incapacitated and what that would mean to
Larry's ministry and business. When you are free-lance,
your income is largely based on what and how much you
produce. There is the occasional hit song or musical or rec-
ord that brings in residuals, but you can't bank on those.
You need a lot of regular, steady work, and you need to
keep hustling and producing. When you're doing your
thing and your wife's thing at the same time, something
suffers. The Mayfields learned hard lessons about getting by
on significantly fewer dollars during those months, and getting back up to speed has been a years-long process.

The next morning an exhausted, short-on-sleep husband and father helped Tracie get Jeff and Shelley fed,
dressed, and off to school. Then he headed for the hospital.
Diane had slept on and off all night. Pastor Reed arrived
early. He said he felt led to share one verse of Scripture
with Diane. He pulled a well-worn Bible from his pocket
and read, "Be still and know that I am God." Then he
prayed and left. Of the jumble of emotions that accompany
a major operation, Diane knew that fear and uncertainty
were her two worst enemies. The verse was perfect. She re-

peated it over and over in her mind as the clock sped toward her appointment with the knife.

Larry helped Diane into the shower. Her first thought upon waking, besides longing for anything that would ease her pain, was that she needed to wash her hair, because she would be out of commission for a few days. She couldn't stand the thought of not being able to wash her hair for so long, so she at least wanted to get that done before surgery. Soon other ministers arrived to pray with them, including the pastor of the Mayfields' previous church, Bill Wilson. Diane felt special and cared for.

She liked and respected Dr. Bradford. She was grateful that God had worked it out that he would be her surgeon. And now, with Pastor Reed's verse echoing in her mind, she felt relaxed and ready to submit to whatever lay ahead.

"Though I was spaced out from all the medication," she says, "I had a deep peace that God was ordering these events and that He would take care of me."

4

Under the Knife

Peace and confidence were wonderful, but they were overridden in Diane's mind by her desperate need to be out of pain. She would agree to, submit to, resign herself to, volunteer for anything that would ease her agony.

When Diane was wheeled off toward the operating room Larry was optimistic, but nervous. He was grateful that Dr. Bradford would be performing the surgery, and he had heard of no life-threatening dangers in this type of an operation. But the myelogram had indicated that a huge piece of disc was pressing on the spinal nerve and might even have become embedded in it. The operation would not be a simple procedure, and Larry watched her disappear down the corridor thinking, *There goes my love. There goes my whole life. God, take care of her.*

Meanwhile, on a golf course in Hot Springs Village, Arkansas, a man stopped his three partners as they approached the tenth tee. "My son-in-law called from Nashville last night to tell me my daughter is going into surgery on her back this morning. The operation will start in about two minutes. Will you pray with me?" With other foursomes waiting behind them, the four knelt near the tee.

Diane thought not only of herself. She also worried about Larry and how difficult it must be for him to be alone just then. But that was just the way Larry wanted it. "I wouldn't have been able to handle anyone staying close, trying to console or encourage me," he says. "I wouldn't have wanted anyone around me at all. Earlier, yes. Later, sure. But while she was in surgery, I didn't want to see any-body, talk to anybody, or even have to say hello to any-body." Having not had breakfast, he went to the cafeteria for a cup of coffee and a sandwich. He took them to the far end, away from anyone else, and ate alone.

He went back to the room, prayed and read Psalm 91, a favorite since childhood: "He that dwelleth in the secret place of the most High shall abide under the shadow of the Almighty. . . . He is my refuge and my fortress: my God; in him will I trust" (vv. 1-2, KJV*). Then he worked on writing musical scores, which was difficult but went all right for a while. Diane was to be gone two hours, and as the time drew near, Larry found it difficult to concentrate. He had been glad for diversions, for something to do, but now it was time to get the word from the doctor, to hear how things had gone, to know how Diane was doing. But there was no word.

Larry fidgeted and paced and prayed some more. He stared out the window. He walked the halls. He wouldn't ask. He knew if there was news he'd be the first to know. He still didn't worry. He simply wondered. What was taking so long? Had there been complications? There was no one to ask. No one knew any more than he did until Dr. Brad-ford would emerge. But when would that be?

An extra half hour became an hour and then an hour and a half. Larry began to sweat. Finally, a full two hours after the surgery was supposed to be over, Dr. Bradford padded down the hall. "Diane is in the recovery room, and she's fine," he said. "I'm sorry it took so long, Larry, but I didn't expect to have to do microsurgery on the nerve. That

* King James Version.

piece from the disc was the biggest I've ever seen, and it was driven into the nerve. It was painstaking work to remove it. One slip and she would have lost the use of her legs. There are no second chances in that kind of surgery."

He explained that he had removed the chip, repaired the nerve, scraped the remaining pulpy tissue from inside the damaged disc, and left the remaining hollow piece in place. "She's extremely vulnerable to further damage. I'm not saying it's going to happen; it probably won't. But now that's it's happened once, it could very well happen again. Make sure she follows my instructions when she gets home. It's vital that she heals properly."

"How long should that take?"

"If she does her part, it could be within six to nine months."

When Diane awoke in the recovery room she was immediately aware of the absence of pressure in her back and pain in her leg. Groggy, foggy, buzzy, she still was happy and relieved. She had no idea how long the operation took, no concept of the complications, and certainly no idea that basically she would be out of commission for the next half to three-quarters of a year. All she knew for sure was that, even in her drugged up, semiconscious state, the pain was gone.

On the way back from the recovery room, with Larry leaning over her, Diane slurred the news, "My leg feels better."

Over the next week, as Diane slowly regained enough strength to be able to go home, Larry drove back and forth between the hospital and home. Tracie spent most of her spring vacation taking care of Jeff and Shelley and being available when they got home from school. Larry drove home late each night to face the chores and the shopping, and also to discover that neighbors provided many meals for the kids.

Diane was overwhelmed by visits and gifts of flowers and food and cards by people from the church and the neighborhood: "If I ever doubted that people cared, that doubt vanished as the days went by." Larry brought the kids to see her occasionally, bringing them up a back elevator.

Larry and Diane were drawn closer together by the ordeal, and even the kids seemed extra tender during this time. Once Diane was back home she was to stay in bed most of the day, except for mealtimes. If she dropped a hair brush, someone else was supposed to pick it up for her. She was on a variety of medications.

And they were making her sick. Members of her Sunday school class prepared, brought, and served complete dinners to the family during her first two weeks at home, yet Diane could sit at the table hardly longer than fifteen minutes. Even then she was unable to eat a bite. Pain, dizziness, and nausea plagued her. "But I did love seeing those friends when they came. I'll never forget the smiles, the kind words, the prayers for my healing."

Her life—the life of the on-the-go suburban housewife and mother—had come to an abrupt halt. She might normally have felt guilty at becoming so reliant on others, especially Larry and the kids, but now she had no choice. They seemed to be more than willing to help out. They even enjoyed it. This was a cause, a mission the whole family had joined.

Besides, maybe God was trying to tell her something. Maybe her expectations had been too great. She knew she had not listened to the messages of pain and fatigue from her body. She had been pushing too much too fast for too long to provide all the activities she thought were best for her family. "Obviously, I had been stopped," she says. "I needed to hear God say, 'Trust Me. Know Me.' "

Their dear friend Bob Benson had come to know what it meant to be forced to stop. Larry and Diane saw him experience several crises in his life, including a battle with cancer. In Bob's words, he had to "regroup, slow down, to simplify, to free up," so that he might learn new and deeper ways of abiding in Christ.

Diane was encouraged as she reread Bob's *In Quest of the Shared Life,* his chronicle of being taken to a place of fear at an inopportune time. To Bob Benson, whatever the price, it was worth it.

"For three months I had to be standing or flat on my back," she says. "When I did sit, I needed a hard-seat chair with a straight back and a cushion to put between my back and the back of the chair. Still, even fifteen minutes sitting was as long as I could take at one time."

Every day Diane promised Larry that she would never do anything again that would put her out of commission like this. "And I promised myself I would never do anything to bring back that horrible pain." Car-pooling was over. Volunteering at school was over. Being everything to her kids was over. Being a perfectionist and having a beautiful home was over.

With his added responsibilities at home, Larry was busier than he had ever been. Though some of his freelance work suffered, he could not let it go completely. They needed his income more than ever, abbreviated though it might be. He was dropping into bed at one or two in the morning and rising at dawn to get started on his daily chores. Yet Diane says she never once heard him complain or blame her for his more difficult life.

Though Diane knew she needed this setting aside, accepting it didn't come all at once. "I was frustrated because the kids had been pretty dependent on me. I couldn't get them ready or help with baths. They could do it themselves, but I had always loved helping."

Still heavily medicated, Diane provided some humor for the family. At meals she might sit there in a daze, nodding, almost toppling forward into her food before Larry helped her back to bed. "Sometimes he would order me back to bed before I had even eaten. He could tell I was nauseated and that I was better off in bed. Drugged up, I was obedient as I could be. He would help me up, point me in the right direction, and walk me down the hall. I loved being in bed."

It was only the pain killers and the muscle relaxants that made it possible for Diane to sit at the table even for short periods, but she was increasingly nauseated every day. Finally she called Dr. Bradford's office and talked to his assistant, Kathy. "Two questions," Diane began. "Could my prescription be making me nauseated?"

"Well, it could. Let me talk to the doctor and see if he wants to change it. I'll have him call you back later today."

"Also, could the trauma of the operation have affected my monthly cycle?"

"That I couldn't say. I'll ask him about that too. Was it early, or are you late?"

"Late."

"How late?"

"About three weeks. It was due about the time of the surgery."

When Dr. Bradford called, he told Diane he would change her medication because of the nausea and that she should have Larry pick up a simple home pregnancy test to rule out potential causes of the interruption of her cycle. "Doctors like to rule out things," she says.

Larry was embarrassed to purchase the pregnancy test from someone he knew, and he wondered what the pharmacist thought was going on in the Mayfield household. Larry didn't even want to think of the possible options.

The pregnancy test was a simple urinalysis associated with a morning specimen, so Diane waited all night before using it. In the morning she carefully placed it atop the file cabinet in Larry's office so no one would jostle it and affect the result. There was no drama in the wait or in the slow trip

50

back to Larry's office to retrieve it. Diane was not hoping or anticipating being pregnant. She was merely ruling out a long-shot possibility to help her doctor determine why she was nauseated and had missed her period.

When the time had passed, Diane slowly moved down the hall and into Larry's empty office. She reached for the vial and held it to the light. She blinked and looked again, and her heart sank. Positive. It wasn't that she didn't want another baby. Diane Mayfield was a baby lover. She had been told she couldn't have children, and then she had loved her adopted daughter fiercely. When God granted her three more pregnancies and two miracle children, she and Larry had felt singularly blessed. She would have more babies today if she thought it was safe and wise. But this was neither. How could she carry a baby nine months when she needed that time to recover? This was a shock, and she was afraid. Could she carry a baby to term? How had this happened? What had she done? What had God done? Her mind flew to the X rays. There had been X rays at the orthopedic doctor's, X rays at the chiropractor, extensive X rays for the myelogram at the hospital for the neurosurgeon. What might she have done to this developing child?

Diane believes that when a woman is pregnant, she can tell. She feels it. And Diane was feeling it. That didn't keep her from also believing, and hoping, that the test result had been inaccurate. But when she told Larry, he was excited. It wasn't that he was blind to the dangers, but they had wanted babies for a long time. "After all we'd been through," Diane says, "you just had to be excited."

So with Larry thrilled and Diane apprehensive—and hoping against the likelihood—she called her obstetrician and made an appointment for that afternoon. It would be her first outing since the surgery.

Getting to the car this time was a whole different story than on March 13. Diane still had to move slowly, especially down the two steps into the garage and getting into the car. But she didn't have to be carried, to hang from Larry's neck, to scream out with every move.

As they headed to the doctor's office, Diane continued to hope she was not pregnant. Down deep, she believed that she was. There was a new closeness between her and Larry and even between her and the kids, all because of the trauma of her back surgery. Maybe this family was ready for an addition. But was she ready for another pregnancy, labor, and birth? "Be still and know that I am God" took on a whole new significance.

5

Advice and Dissent

Diane felt conspicuous in the waiting room of Dr. Cummings.* The place was filled with husbands and vivacious wives in their twenties. Here she was, almost thirty-nine and fresh from back surgery, which she was trying to camouflage. She turned in her specimen, and when she was called in to see the doctor she walked slowly but as smoothly as possible.

Diane was waiting in an examining room when Dr. Cummings arrived. "One way to avoid PMS," he said, "is to get pregnant."

She smiled. "Don't you know this is serious?"

He nodded. "Let's have a look." As he examined her he said, "You're about seven weeks along. And what's this?"

He had discovered the battery-operated machine attached to her back and designed to confuse the nerve endings and reduce pain. She had the feeling he was amused by it, but for her it worked. Then he asked a lot of questions about her back, the operation, the incision. "The pregnancy is not going to harm your back. By the time you start getting big, you'll be through the first six months since the oper-

* Not his real name.

53

ation. If you do what you're supposed to do and don't do what you're not supposed to do, you should be able to carry the baby and deliver with no problem."

"But what about all the medication, the X rays?" Diane asked, thinking he sounded a little too matter-of-fact.

He didn't answer immediately. He sat down. "In my opinion, if there was chromosomal damage, the baby will spontaneously abort, just like your previous miscarriage."

That was a bit of a relief to Diane, but if there *was* chromosomal damage, she would have felt guilty about the medication and the X rays. Of course she never would have had them deliberately, had she known she was pregnant, but still, she says, "It would have been awful."

Diane told Dr. Cummings that because of her back, she and Larry had not been intimate more than once in the last two months. He smiled, and she could have mouthed his response with him: "It only takes once."

When Diane returned to the waiting room, Larry could tell by the look on her face that she was pregnant. She said nothing in front of the other patients, but when they were outside, she confirmed that it was true. Larry was happy. All the way home, he smiled, making her feel good about the pregnancy, too.

As soon as they arrived home, Diane got rid of all her medicines and decided to go off painkillers cold turkey. All she would use from that point on was the electronic machine, which she turned up to high strength. "I got used to it and didn't even take aspirin after that."

She called and broke the news of her pregnancy to Dr. Bradford, whom she was to see the following week for her four weeks' postoperative check-up. He said he would talk to her about it at that time. When the time came, Larry and Diane met with the doctor in an examining room at the same hospital where the surgery had been performed. Diane changed into a hospital gown and sat on the examining table. Larry sat in a chair nearby as Dr. Bradford gently checked the incision and her spine.

"How've you been doing?" he asked. "Everything all right?"

"Under the circumstances," Diane said, smiling. "Of course I've been off medication since my visit to Dr. Cummings."

"Uh-huh. Your back looks good. It seems to be coming along fine." He pulled up a chair. "I need to talk to you now." Larry and Diane stole a glance at each other, but their smiles froze as the kind doctor spoke matter-of-factly, as if recommending a throat culture. "I really feel you need an abortion right away."

Diane wanted to blurt, "We don't believe in abortion," but she wanted to hear him out. He had been so kind, so generous. He had taken her as a patient virtually off the street, and his work in the operation had been magnificent. She knew he cared about her.

"It's too big a gamble," he said. "Others of my patients have found themselves in the same situation, and sixty percent have chosen to abort. The fetus was four weeks old at the time you had the myelogram and the radiation, not to mention all the medication and the operation itself."

Seeing their noncommittal looks, he told them of a baby "in neonatal surgery in this hospital right now who was born under similar circumstances. The baby was born with two brains and will not likely survive. The head is severely deformed, and the outlook is bleak. I wouldn't want you to have to face that with all you've gone through."

I'm not a statistic, Diane thought. *I am a person, and I'm carrying a child.*

"Seeing deformed babies is what drove me from obstetrics," Dr. Bradford continued. "I was an obstetrician in North Carolina, and I just couldn't take any more of that tragedy."

"We don't believe in abortion," Diane said kindly.

"Oh, don't misunderstand me," Dr. Bradford said. "I don't either, morally. I especially detest it as a form of birth control or as a convenience. The abortion mills in North Carolina were another factor in my decision to change my field to neurology. Few doctors are as opposed to abortion as I am, morally and religiously. I'm speaking to you medically, practically, from the standpoint of the percentages and the likelihood of what you will undoubtedly encounter. Your baby was four to six inches away from that X-ray machine at a very critical stage in his development. His brain stem and nervous system were being developed. The odds are that we have caused severe damage. I am urging you to make the decision and make it quickly—as soon as possible, even today."

The room felt icy. The doctor left as quickly as he had entered, having left no opportunity for discussion. Clearly he had thought this through, and there was no question in his mind. Larry and Diane looked at each other, unable to speak. On each other's faces they read the same message. *There's no way. No way we can get an abortion.* They didn't even want to think about it, but it would have been easier to pass off if the doctor had grown horns and admitted that he was some abortionist butcher. This was their doctor, their kind, gentle, compassionate, basically pro-life doctor. He was the one who had rescued Diane, had put her back together, relieved her pain, saved her from paralysis.

Babies with cleft palates could be linked to X rays. So could babies born with spina bifida. What if they gave birth to a deformed child and Diane was injured in the process? Could Larry be expected to take care of two invalids for the rest of his life?

Their knee-jerk reaction was swift, but when it came to fleshing it out, to really thinking about the ramifications, that was a whole new subject. They knew they couldn't have an abortion. To them it was a matter of obedience to the Word of God. To them, abortion was murder. But neither was it an easy matter to conclude and drop.

"We talked about it a lot," Diane says. "Life is sacred to us. We see God as the Creator, the giver of life. We could not take the life He had so obviously placed within me. That was the bottom line: we couldn't do it. We knew before we walked out of that office that we would try to have this baby. I confess I prayed that if anything was wrong with it, God would allow it to miscarry. But for the same reason we didn't take fertility pills when we were told we should, we thought it would be tampering to invade the sanctity of the womb by aborting, too.

"In my humanness, I was afraid. I found myself wanting an abortion at times. I wanted to be free of something that might cripple me or change our lives too drastically, were the baby handicapped. I understood the fear that grips any young girl facing a pregnancy out of wedlock.

"The Lord was patient with me because He knew I would obey Him and carry the baby to term if at all possible. As for Larry, he never wavered in his conviction that we had to do the right thing. He did, however, look at the whole issue of abortion with deeper insight. It is one thing to decry abortion with a programmed—albeit right—response. It's another to have to face it head on."

In truth, though their minds were made up and the matter seemed settled, Diane went through tremendous turmoil for the next several months. Both credit Dr. Bradford for accepting their decision, wishing them the best, and never again raising an objection to her carrying the child to term. But in Diane's own mind, the battle raged.

While Larry became "Mr. Mom," to the delight of the kids, who called him that everyday (he laughed with them and accepted his role), Diane had small and large tasks to accomplish each day. Her small ones were reading and writing to friends. Larry also involved her in choosing songs for a children's album, *Kids Sing Praise*.

Her large task was to accept what lay before her. It was a process that would take months. In the past, because she had been raised by devout parents in a solid Christian home, she had believed she had all the answers. She had been a Christian since childhood, had attended Bible college, and had experienced God's seeing her through the tragedy of the loss of her brother and her baby, and also leading her through many triumphs. She could say she accepted the current situation, that she believed God and trusted Him with all of it, but more often than she cares to remember, she found herself slipping and looking only at her circumstances and not to the God who controls all circumstances.

Diane had the feeling that before they started announcing to everyone she was pregnant she had to sort through all of that and know in her heart that she was doing the right thing. She feared the response of her children. Would they be embarrassed, react negatively? What about her friends, the ones who made snide comments about others her age who turned up pregnant?

She and Larry told both sets of parents and Diane's sister, Julie. All were supportive and promised to pray. Julie had recently begun counseling in a crisis pregnancy center, and Diane became her first counselee with a crisis pregnancy. The mother of four girls and a pastor's wife, she was unusually thrilled about Diane's impending child. Julie faithfully encouraged Diane with already familiar Scripture —Psalm 100:3 and Jeremiah 1:5. At first Diane didn't want to think about the verses' applying to her, but eventually the Word that will not return void gradually penetrated her callousness and took hold in her soul. She was glad that her own sister could be her personal long-distance counselor. Julie told her other counselees about Diane and Larry's decision, and Diane hopes that the news may have spared the lives of other children.

Scripture began to mean more than ever to Diane as she lay flat on her back most of the day. She was thrilled anew with Psalm 37, which she had discovered as a Bible school student and which promised her the desires of her heart if she delighted herself in the Lord. It also urged her to recommit her way to the Lord and to be still without fretting. She appreciated Proverbs 10:24 as well, which promised that "what the righteous desire will be granted." "I knew God counted me righteous," she says, "not because of anything I had done or not done but because of what Christ had done on my behalf."

Diane believes she reached another turning point in her struggle when she read Mark 9:37, in which Jesus says, "Whoever welcomes one of these little children in my name, welcomes me . . ." It reminded her of when she was thirteen and worked a summer with Down's Syndrome children. She found herself eager to be with those children and discovered she received more love and acceptance from them than she could give. She found true love for them in her heart.

She also read Charles Swindoll's book *Compassion*, in which he spoke to the same issue. A woman in his church had two severely handicapped children, who provided the church the opportunity to love them as if they were loving Christ. Diane came to the conclusion that if her child was born handicapped, he would provide an opportunity for God's people to minister to Christ Himself.

Psalm 139 became a cornerstone for Larry's and Diane's personal prayer life. Every morning they met together and claimed the truth that the body that was being formed within Diane was fearfully and wonderfully made, that it was being knit together in secret in her innermost parts.

They made it a point to pray for that unborn child every day during her pregnancy, specifically asking God to do

His perfect will in creating every minute detail. From finger-nails and tiny toes to kidneys, liver, limbs, and hair, they prayed and prayed as the days rolled by.

Still, Diane harbored a very real fear that people would not understand. She wasn't ready for anyone else to know. Not her pastor, not her children, not her friends, not her church or Sunday school class. She prayed about that, too, knowing that she would have to be strong, to be convinced she was doing the right thing, so that no matter what their reaction, she could face it, own up to it, accept it.

She knew that once she told her children the news, it would spread quickly. Yet she couldn't hold off for long. Already Shelley—who came up to her waistline—had once noticed her tummy and asked, "Mommy, are you pregnant?"

"How would you feel about it if I was?"

"Oh, I'd love to have a baby! Please have a baby!"

By May Jeff was wondering why recuperating from back surgery would give his mother a craving for *Dr Pepper* and fried chicken. She knew he would love her to have a baby too, because he often talked about his friends who had little brothers.

She worried most about Tracie. Could a teenager get excited about her mother's being pregnant? Or would she think it was gross and embarrassing? When an acquaintance of the family had a baby at forty, Tracie thought it was horrible because when the baby grew up the parents would be too old. Diane couldn't understand why teenagers think growing old is such a curse. When she was a child older people were revered. "The world is such a confused, backward place now," she decided, and she worried all the more about the reaction Tracie might have.

"I just knew Tracie would be embarrassed, and so I was concerned about her. I didn't want her to think that with this baby we were infringing on her freedom to enjoy being a teenager. I knew being a teenager is a special time to look forward to, and I didn't want to get in the way of that at all. She was the only one of our kids with her own room, and she had to wonder where we would put another child."

Those were just some of the fears and unknowns Diane was working through, trying to control the situation and get comfortable with the idea of people beginning to know. She knew the longer she went without telling anyone, the harder it would be when they found out.

Once she felt she had gone through her own total acceptance, including the possibility of delivering a handicapped child, she and Larry decided to make their announcement to the children on Diane's thirty-ninth birthday: June 3, 1985.

6

The News

One of the things that had made the acceptance process so difficult for Diane and which, in fact, forced her to repeat that acceptance afresh everyday, was a bombardment of bad news about pregnancies. It seemed everywhere she turned, someone her age was having a baby born with severe complications. She heard of Down's Syndrome children, stillbirths, and spina bifida, and she read of dozens more. Accepting those possibilities was not a once-for-all proposition. She needed to recommit herself to God daily and renew her attitude of faith and compliance.

Dr. Cummings strongly urged her to undergo amniocentesis, a process involving the removal of a small amount of fluid from the amniotic sac for study. Both Larry and Diane hated the idea, believing that the womb is sacred and shouldn't be intruded upon. They had also read and heard that the test itself can be dangerous and potentially more harmful than the maladies it's supposed to detect. Anyway, they reasoned, since they had planned to accept whatever might be wrong with this child, what was the point of knowing in advance? They would not abort regardless, so what was the point?

The test was scheduled for a week after they had planned to tell the children, and though they both were uncomfortable with it, neither had made a final decision not to go through with the procedure. As Diane's birthday approached, they planned to make the amniocentesis part of what they wanted the kids to pray for. The time had come for the whole ordeal to become a joint venture of prayer for the family. They were eager for the kids to know and be involved.

It's a Mayfield family tradition that Larry and the kids serve Diane breakfast in bed on her birthday. They bring the tray and climb onto the bed with her. On this morning Shelley sat next to her on one side. Jeff was at her feet. Tracie sat in the rocking chair and Larry on the edge of the bed. After lots of fun and joking, Larry said, "Mom has something very important to tell you."

Diane looked at each child before she spoke, letting her silence and their attention add weight and import to the moment. "God has blessed our family," she said. "I'm going to have a baby, and—"

But she couldn't continue. She couldn't say she needed and wanted their support and acceptance and prayers. It wasn't because she had become emotional and couldn't speak. It was because she would not have been heard over the din. Instantaneously all three children had burst into cheers. They laughed and giggled and shouted with delight. Diane felt total acceptance from all three, and she was overwhelmed. "All my worries about their reactions dissipated in that moment of their total acceptance. It was a healing moment for me. Immediately, I knew everything would be all right. God used that special moment.

"After we laughed and cried over the news, I told them of the risks, of the odds against my having a perfectly healthy baby. I told them of the important test we faced at the end of the week. I wanted them to know everything, to be with us through it all. 'We can't do this alone,' I told them. 'We need you to face this with us as a family.' "

Diane (left) tried to hide her back and leg pain from Shelley, Tracie, and Jeff, but the family's brief trip to Gatlinburg was nearly ruined by it.

From left: Shelley, Jeff, Diane, and Tracie.

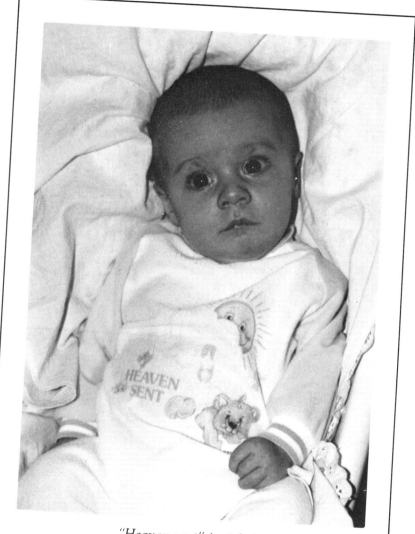

"Heaven sent" is right!

Diane with Jonathan.

Larry with Jonathan.

Tracie with Jonathan.

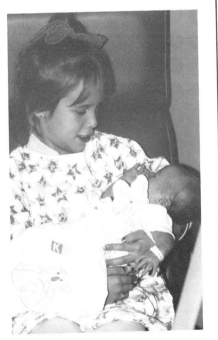

Shelley with Jonathan.

Jeff with Jonathan.

The kids are thrilled.

On Sunday, February 16, Larry and Diane Mayfield presented Jonathan Brian to Pastor Reed in dedication to the Lord. Pictured L to R: Larry, Diane holding Jonathan, Pastor Reed and Tracie; front: Shelley and Jeff.

From left: Jeff, Diane, Jonathan, Shelley, Larry, and Tracie.

From left: Jonathan, Diane, Shelley, Tracie, and Jeff on Mother's Day, 1989.

Jeff, Jonathan, Larry, Diane, Tracie, and Shelley.

Larry suggested that each child pray for his new brother or sister. "It was wonderful to hear their prayers," Diane says.

That day Diane realized afresh the faith of a child. Little Shelley spoke with the wisdom of one who had never faced severe disappointments. Her faith was complete. She said without equivocation, "God wouldn't have put the baby in you if it wasn't going to be OK."

Diane smiled at her daughter's simplistic response. She thought of the years she had prayed for her brother Brian and how he had died anyway. She thought of the years she and Larry and others had prayed about the severe, constant pain in Larry's knees and how God had not chosen to heal him or even to relieve the pain. She knew that when you've lived longer and have seen prayers that have not been answered the way you wished, your faith can be affected.

Diane looked at her unblinking daughter, tempted to tell her that though faith is real and important and impossible to live without, sometimes we don't get the answers we pray for. But there was something appealing and engaging about this child and her childlike faith. She had stated her belief without hesitation, and Diane could not—would not—attempt to neutralize her faith. Instead of saying, "Well, Shelley, it doesn't always turn out the way we hope or pray or believe," Diane chose at that moment to embrace her daughter's faith.

"I did," she recalls. "I chose. Faith is a decision. You choose to believe, decide to believe. I appropriated Shelley's faith for my own."

Jeff is the Mayfields' compliant child, very accepting. He's their peace in the midst of the storm. Even his name means peace, though they didn't know that when they named him. Jeff thought the news of a new brother or sister was awesome. He just knew it would be a brother and that he would finally have someone to play with, someone to teach about sports.

Diane's fears about Tracie's reaction disappeared when Tracie said, "When can I go shopping with you for maternity clothes?"

Diane was invigorated. She felt she could face the world now. Her family was behind her 100 percent, and she was ready to move on, to tell her friends, even the ones whose reactions she feared. She even felt she could face the amniocentesis, and she explained that to the kids.

Next on the list of those who needed to know was the Mayfields' pastor. "We wanted him to know and to affirm us," Diane says. "He had been there before I went into surgery. He had been with me before any of us knew I was carrying a child. We wanted his support and his prayers."

Pastor Millard Reed admitted to Larry and Diane that when he got their call asking for an appointment he wondered if there was trouble in the marriage because of the trauma of a wife who was temporarily an invalid. Or maybe Larry and Diane needed advice on a career change. He didn't know. "It's clear," he said, "that God has already advised you about your situation by leading you to ask your pastor to stand with you. I feel honored and appreciated." He commented many times, to them and later to others, that the Mayfields had not asked him whether they should have the baby: "They told me they had decided to have it. God had already counseled them."

The pastor assured Larry and Diane that the church would be behind them. He prayed for them and told them of a recent speaking engagement in a home for handicapped children. "It was poignant," he said, "and having a handicapped child is a very real possibility you have to face. You won't face it alone, however."

One more time before the amniocentesis at the end of that week Diane told Dr. Cummings, "I don't really need or want this, because we have decided to keep the baby, no matter what."

"I understand," he said. "But it's a high-risk pregnancy. Let's do it so we can eliminate some possibilities."

Diane knew that even if the test showed she was carrying a Down's Syndrome child or one with spina bifida, she would not abort. If that knowledge helped the doctor in the delivery process, she guessed that was OK, though with their enormous medical bills, she wished they didn't have to go to the expense of the test. "Yet I wanted to be submissive to my doctor," she says. "I was ready to face it. Or I thought I was."

On the way to the clinic, Larry and Diane tried to think about what lay before them. Diane wanted to turn around and go home. And they almost did. Larry had been against the test from the beginning. "What is the use of having this test when we're going to keep the baby anyway?" he asked. "It's a lousy test. The risks alone—"

At the clinic Diane put the question to the doctor again. "It'll just help you to face whatever's out there," he said.

"Which is what we'd been doing all along," Diane recalls. "But I really did trust him. He had delivered Shelley and had seen us through our miscarriage. I was reassured to know that he would be performing the test, not just some technician."

The morning began with an ultrasound where Larry and Diane got to see images of the baby moving in her womb. That briefly took their minds off the impending amniocentesis. They saw the tiny heart beating rapidly and steadily. "That was thrilling," Diane says. "This was just before my second trimester, so we had already been monitoring the heartbeat during my regular visits to Dr. Cummings's office. But to see it on the screen, and for Larry to see it, that was great."

They could not detect the sex of the baby, but they could see the spine. The doctor said all the limbs were there and seemed in good proportion to the spine and skull. "The doctor's good words about the baby were wonderful to our ears," Diane says. "The ultrasound was great, and I lay there thinking that this trip was worth it for that alone. I was ready for the amniocentesis. I wasn't happy about it, but I was resigned to it."

As the doctor checked her abdomen for the position of the baby, however, he hesitated. He spoke with a technician, then announced that he wouldn't be able to perform the amniocentesis because the placenta was on top and he could not risk going through it. Diane grinned. "I was so relieved! It was wonderful! It was as if God was saying that He wanted us to trust Him completely and to not eliminate or seek to know if there were any problems to consider. He wanted to assure me I could trust Him totally and not to look at or rely upon tests. I was to look solely to Him. I went out of there hilarious."

Larry was convinced more than ever that God had placed that baby in her womb. "She had gotten pregnant when physically she probably shouldn't have, and now God clearly wanted us to trust Him and not to worry about it."

The kids loved the photograph from the ultrasound. Diane was still early in her pregnancy, and even though the limbs and spine and skull looked good, there was no telling what the brain and brain stem and nervous system looked like. According to Dr. Bradford, the Mayfields had every likelihood of having a severely brain damaged child.

Next on Larry and Diane's agenda was to break the news to their Sunday school class. Larry told the teacher, Bob Benson, that Diane wanted to say a few words of appreciation to the group.

The class of about forty seemed pleased to see Diane back in circulation, still walking slowly but able to get around. She began her remarks by thanking the class for its

68

many expressions of love and concern to her and to her husband and family. "Your cards and letters and gifts of food were overwhelming," she said. "Knowing I have friends who love me like you do has been a big part of my healing process."

She went on to tell some details of her injury, her operation, her recuperation. She spoke of how Larry and the kids pitched in, how he had taken over many of her duties, even on top of his own busy schedule. She thanked them again for all they had meant to her. Then she said, "And now I have another bit of news for you . . ."

7

Requiem for Fear

First gasps, then tears came when Diane told her Sunday school class she was pregnant. She told them the whole story and let them know they were among the very first, after family and pastor, to be informed. "I need your prayers for the rest of my pregnancy, just like you stood by me through my surgery."

After class, Bob Benson, who had five kids of his own, his youngest being a senior in high school, said, "Just think, now *you* can be the oldest parents at graduation!"

One of the delights of that class was the involvement of Bob Benson. He was a creative, funny man who was also deep and spiritual. He would be dead of cancer within a year, but in the meantime he continued to encourage Larry and Diane.

Not one person in that class remarked about Diane's being pregnant during surgery, nor did anyone make a comment about her becoming pregnant at her age. They could see that God had prepared her for any eventuality, and they began a prayer vigil that would last as long as she carried her child. The women Diane had worried the most about, the ones she feared might be her critics, proved to be the most supportive. She believes God prepared them for the news. "It helped to be able to tell them my story and have them agree that God was doing something special with me. I learned more and more with each day that Isaiah 55:8 is true: 'For my thoughts are not your thoughts, neither are your ways my ways, declares the Lord.'

"Another passage that meant a lot to me during that time was 2 Corinthians 1:9-11: 'Indeed, in our hearts we felt the sentence of death. But this happened that we might not rely on ourselves but on God, who raises the dead. He has delivered us from such a deadly peril, and He will deliver us. On Him we have set our hope that He will continue to deliver us, as you help us by your prayers.' "

Diane felt blessed that not only did the friends in her Sunday school class not criticize her but they accepted her and supported her and agreed with her that God was doing something special. "They knew God was in it, that I had accepted it, and they wanted to be part of the journey."

For some reason, Diane became more sensitive to handicapped children. They seemed to glow like neon signs wherever she went. She was certain there weren't more of them around than there had ever been, but now she didn't miss one. She noticed the young mother in Penney's who struggled to control her cerebral palsied daughter. She wondered, *How would I do that?* She was resigned to the fact that she could very well have a child just like that, but how, with her back, would she be able to handle it? In her mind there was no one more courageous than the parent of a handicapped child.

It was as if God were preparing her for whatever lay ahead. She saw handicapped kids on the street, in cars, everywhere. She knew God would give her the courage she needed if she was called to be the mother of such a child. Yet she and Larry prayed all the more that their baby would be healthy.

People in the various prayer groups supporting them also prayed that if anything had already happened to the brain, brain stem, or nervous system, God would heal it before birth. Larry and Diane prayed over and over, "Lord answer this prayer and give us a normal, healthy baby and we will never ask for another thing again." They smile now at that and how it seems to fly in the face of their acceptance of whatever God had in store for them. "But we were honest," Larry says. "We were happy to take what God gave us, and we knew He would give us the strength to handle whatever came our way, but yes, of course we wanted a perfect baby."

Diane says that they were following the admonition in Hebrews 4:16: "Let us then approach the throne of grace with confidence, so that we may receive mercy and find grace to help us in our time of need." Just as they marveled at what might have come of Diane's surgery—the impact not hitting them until they were home and realized what it would have been like with her as an invalid—they wanted to leave God room to perform a miracle with their baby too. Resigned to a handicapped child, yes, but all the while believing and trusting that God could also give them a perfect baby.

Most of all, they promised God that they would tell far and wide the story of His faithfulness, regardless how the baby turned out. They also prayed for their other children, being careful not to put so much emphasis on the unborn child that the others were left out. They have continued their daily, morning vigil of prayer for each of their children. They pray about their entire days, what they might face at school and with their friends, their protection, their guidance, their spiritual growth.

Diane was especially impressed by Tracie's attitude throughout the pregnancy. One day Diane asked her, "If something is wrong with the baby, how will that affect you?"

"If there's something wrong with it, it will just need more love, and we'll have more love to give it."

As the summer wore on, Diane began to feel like a misfit. She was getting bigger, and though her back was stronger and she was able to get out more, she didn't know where she belonged. When she went to the pool with friends her age, they sat talking about braces and sports and dates for their children. Across the way were the pregnant women in their twenties, discussing bottles and formulas and diapers.

The daughter of one of Diane's friends became pregnant out of wedlock and decided to carry the child to term. Diane admired her for that, but what a strange sensation it was to be pregnant at the same time as this child, the daughter of a friend her own age!

Even though that baby was conceived out of wedlock, the result of a mistake, God was knitting its parts in secret and had a purpose for it too. Diane stayed close to her friend throughout the ordeal and watched with interest as the daughter grew larger and made preparations to have the child adopted. The baby was due several months before Diane's.

The baby came late, and Diane called the hospital for news. The girl had delivered a boy, but he was on a respirator. He had just a brain stem, no brain, and would not live apart from the machine. Diane was devastated, thinking of her friend and her friend's daughter. And was this yet another message, a bit of divine preparation for what she herself would face? She couldn't let herself think about that. She must not. She threw herself into praying for her friend and caring for that family. What could she do? How should she react? Would she go to the funeral? She must.

The service was held in a small, beautiful church, and Diane was, at first, glad they had come. But the sadness of the occasion pressed in. The little sister of the baby's mother, happy to see Larry and Diane, confided in them, "I brought a teddy bear to put in the casket." Even the adoptive parents were there. They had been at the hospital for

74

the birth, ready to see their new child as soon as he was born. And now he rested in a little white casket at the front of the church. Diane did not see how she could file past that open coffin with the rest of the congregation at the close of the service. It was too much for her.

She forced her mind to wander to the day at school recently when a teacher patted her on the back and said, "You're so brave!" Brave was something she was not. Faithful. Trusting. Accepting. Resigned, maybe. But brave? She didn't feel brave. "I felt I was hanging from a precipice." She had been encouraged and admonished through Scripture to look at God and not at circumstances, but every day, it seemed, Satan threw some new circumstance at her. She could find true peace resting in God until she thought about the statistics or heard about problem births or saw handicapped children. "God had put this baby within me, and I was troubled that I wasn't as fully excited as I should have been. Yet I knew this was God's will and that He was there with me."

Diane had tried not to express her doubts and fears about her pregnancy because she felt pressure to appear faithful. So to others, she *did* appear brave. But this funeral would be the test. Could she take it in stride—or even appear to? The grandmother of this tragic baby was her friend. Diane wanted to be there for her and to be supportive. Could she push from her mind the turmoil, the terror, the devastation of grief that washed over her for this tiny, innocent victim? Had she done the same to the child within her by carelessly rushing in to X rays, myelogram, surgery? God knows she hadn't done any of that on purpose. And what choice did she have anyway? The pain would have killed her—baby or no baby. What could she have done? What precautions could she have taken?

The service was sweet with singing and Scripture, but then Psalm 139 was read. There was no mention of the fact that though God had knit this child in his mother's womb, he had not turned out perfectly. Diane had been claiming that very passage as a source of strength, and now it was used at the funeral of a baby born with no brain.

When the service was over, sure enough, the ushers directed the congregation, row by row, to file to the front and past the casket. Could they slip out? Would they be noticed? Of course they would. Would people understand? Surely they would. But could Diane take that chance? Did she want to appear weak, unsupportive? The ushers drew nearer. She was nearly in a panic.

"Lord, give me strength," she breathed. Larry followed her to the front, where she briefly looked at the baby then turned to her friend and to her friend's daughter. She expressed her sympathy, offered her help, and said the baby looked precious. The family wept. Diane held her breath and made her way out of the church, feeling as if she had earned a victory of sorts. She had held together. She had buried the early fears about her own child. She had turned her attention to loved ones who hurt, and she was able to convince herself once and for all that she had accepted her fate. Whatever God brought to her would be fine. She would handle it. No problem.

She thought.

On the way to the car they chatted with other friends, and Diane had calmed. She was able to engage in small talk and answer questions about her own condition. She had successfully pushed her deep-seated fears to the recesses of her mind and could now concentrate on the last four months of her pregnancy. Onward and upward were her goals. She felt better physically, convinced herself she was doing better psychologically, and slept well that night.

In the morning she received a call from her dear friend Wanda from church. Wanda was a woman in her Sunday school class who believed deeply in the power of intercessory prayer. It was Wanda who had started the Sunday school class prayer chain. But this morning she was not informing Diane of a prayer request. She was, instead, telling her of a leading from the Spirit she had received.

"The Lord told me you needed prayer," she said cheerfully, "so I called to find out what's the matter."

"Well, Wanda, nothing's the matter. I'm fine. I feel good. Larry and I had our time in the Word this morning and in prayer for the kids. We're claiming Psalm 139, so—"

"Has anything happened?" Wanda pressed kindly. "The Lord really impressed me to call because you had a need in your life."

Wanda had always been very sensitive to the Spirit, but Diane still had herself convinced that things were fine. She wasn't aware what was happening in her subconscious. "No," Diane said, "matter of fact yesterday we went to the funeral of a grandbaby of a friend of mine." She told Wanda all about the situation and the service and how she felt God had given her victory. "I felt brave in that I could be a comfort to them, because we're told in Scripture to comfort the comfortless and the sorrowing."

"Oh, I just knew there was something," Wanda said. "The Holy Spirit wants to heal your subconscious from all that worry. Let me pray for you right now."

And she did. Slowly Diane began to realize that Wanda had indeed been led by God to call her. When Diane hadn't been aware of her own need, God had laid it on Wanda's heart. When Wanda finished praying, she told Diane of her experience of having lost a nine-month-old baby herself. "It was hard," she said, "and we couldn't have survived without the Lord. But you know, God used that to lead my husband to Christ. He received the Lord, praying over our baby's grave."

Suddenly everything in Diane broke loose. She wept and told Wanda her true feelings at the funeral, all the fears and the desperation, how badly she wanted to truly accept whatever God had for her but how she longed for a perfect baby. Wanda understood and prayed with her again.

Diane still sees that as a major turning point in the entire experience. She felt cleansed from the inside out. She knew it would have been unhealthy for her to bottle up all those feelings and fears and pretend she was fine when she wasn't. Now that they were all out in the open, confessed, prayed about, and dealt with, she felt she could go on and face anything.

She would never again pretend to be at peace when she wasn't. She would work toward total acceptance and remain fully honest about the desires of her heart. She wanted a perfect baby, and she was afraid that was impossible. But that was truth she could handle and live with.

8
The Home Stretch

Diane is convinced that intercessory prayer became the Mayfields' lifeline. She noticed in her conversation with Wanda that the more she confessed, the more she felt led to confess. She remembered reading in *Key to a Loving Heart*, by her friend Karen Mains, that the human heart was described as having multiple doors that lead to each other. "You might open the first or second door," Diane says, "but there are always more and deeper doors that need to be opened so that all can be bared to the Lord. God needed to become Lord of my entire situation. The verses that meant the most to me just then were James 1:2-4: 'Consider it pure joy, my brothers, whenever you face trials of many kinds, because you know that the testing of your faith develops perseverance. Perseverance must finish its work so that you may be mature and complete, not lacking anything.' "

Intercessory prayer became the catalyst God used to work His way more deeply into Larry and Diane's lives. "It really changed us," she says. They began getting more and more reminders in the mail that people were praying for them. The more they learned about the value of such prayer, the more they were open and shared their needs with the prayer chain from Zion, Illinois, the prayer group from church, with relatives in Arkansas, friends in California and Texas—all over the country.

It was also during that time, in late July and early August, that Larry was asked to lead a time of singing and praise on Wednesday nights. Before the pastor spoke and people began the prayer meeting Larry led a time of worship from the piano and shared thoughts from the Word. Sometimes he began sentence prayers or asked for testimonies around a central truth. It was all planned, but his goal was to make it come off as impromptu. He was also ready to let the worship period take its own course if he felt something was happening that was more meaningful than what he had planned.

Through that and other formal and informal leadership opportunities, more people in the church got to know Larry and Diane and learned of their situation. Of course, with the Sunday school class knowing the story, it soon began to spread. But the day came when the pastor felt it would be important for the congregation to hear the story directly, together and all at the same time.

So Larry told the story, and the congregation responded with such an outpouring of prayer and support and encouragement that Diane was amazed. "We hadn't been at the church for very long, and I was surprised that people would be so willing to pray for us," she says. "It's kind of sad. Perhaps we didn't feel worthy of it."

"We hadn't been the recipients of so much prayer before," Larry says. "We'd never thought of needing it that much."

Larry kept the Wednesday night crowd abreast of the situation after that, and they so loved what he was doing that they devoted part of each service to pray for Diane and the baby. Larry became a sort of folk hero to the group because he always seemed to bring them something close to what the pastor's twenty-minute message would be on. Pastor Reed also believed the Spirit was guiding Larry in that.

While the church was upholding them in prayer, so were dear friends and loved ones from all over the United States. Their closest friends from Moody days, Sherm and Marti Williams and their children, spent a few days with them in August. Larry and Diane had knelt and prayed with these friends when the Williamses had left Chicago to move to California. Now Larry, Sherm, and Marti laid hands on Diane and prayed for her. Then Sherm and Marti took their story back to the choir at the Fremont (California) Community Church where many prayed. In September, when Diane might be at a low ebb, she would receive notes of encouragement from people out there she had neither met nor even heard of. They would affirm her decision to go through with the pregnancy and assure her of their prayers that God's will would be done.

In Zion, Illinois, where Larry's parents lived, the prayer chain at Grace Missionary Church took up the cause. Diane was most impressed by Grace member Connie Birky Edwards, whom she describes as "the best example of the all-American, beautiful homemaker, mother, and active church member I have ever known. She loved her husband, her two teenagers, and her Lord Jesus."

Just in her mid-forties, Mrs. Edwards had contracted ALS, better known as Lou Gehrig's disease. She would die that September, two months before Diane was due, but Diane recalls that "she never lost her radiance or her spirit. And she prayed for me and my baby right to the end. It is so humbling."

In Hot Springs Village, Arkansas, Diane's parents met with a new group of believers. Every Wednesday afternoon at about five, Diane's mother called to see if Diane had any specific prayer requests. The people in that church prayed not only for Diane and the unborn child, but also for each of the other children.

The bigger the baby grew the more difficult it became for Diane to be comfortable. She had to lie on her side most of the time because the weight of the baby would have pressed down too heavily on the damaged disc if she lay on her back.

As fall approached, Diane was unable to attend the Wednesday night services at church, so Larry took notes and told her all about them on their frequent walks. Diane was frustrated that she couldn't even replant her own tulip garden as she had done every fall before that. She felt useless, but she didn't feel hopeless. She felt buoyed up by all the prayer being lifted on her behalf. "It was like being a few feet off the ground. These were priceless times, encouraging both of us, showing us how God was again using His people to strengthen us with His truth."

At least twice Larry came home with stories that brought tears to Diane's eyes. One was from a young man in the church who said he had shared the Mayfields' story with a young pregnant woman at work, and she had decided not to abort her baby. Also, the wife of songwriter Jon Mohr, who attended the same church, said Jon's mother had been told to abort him because his was a high-risk pregnancy. Jon was born healthy and went on to become a servant of God through his music, writing, and performing.

Seven and a half months into her pregnancy, Diane was seeing the days drag by. It was all she could do to walk a mile, and it took much more time than she was used to. It was about all the exercise she could handle. Here was a woman who had loved and enjoyed her previous pregnancies. She had been vibrant, radiant, full of extra energy, eager to prove that a pregnant woman could do everything and more than the normal woman. But now she was under it, trying to recuperate from back surgery without medication, that recovery slowed due to the extra weight. The summer days were hot and lazy, and the clock seemed to stand still.

"I asked myself," she says, "how I could face not being able to do what I was used to doing. I was accustomed to ordering my life, using my gifts for the Lord, striving to become all I could be—all He wanted me to be. I wanted my strong body back so I could be Super Mom and do all those great things experts write books about. I wanted my children to rise up and call me wonderful, but all they did was rise up and call me!"

Forced to have many quiet moments, Diane lay in her bedroom and watched the leaves fall from the maple trees in the back yard. She contemplated the verse God had given her at the beginning of the year. It was time to determine what that new thing was He had promised them in that passage. She had long since realized it would not be television work as they had hoped. As is common with such projects, it was put on hold—and Larry would not have had the time to devote to it anyway. It might still happen, Diane realized, but it was already forgotten for 1985.

Diane had practiced integrating Scripture into her days for most of her life. She had grown up in a good Christian home, had gone to a great Bible school, had served with her husband in various creative and effective ministries, and was humbled to know that God had used Larry and her to accomplish some of His purposes. But now, she decided, those formulas for successful Christian living had to be taken to Jesus and laid at His feet. "I had to face a different way of thinking and living."

She knew deep within that God had something good in this for her. The truth of Jeremiah 29:11 rang in her heart: " 'For I know the plans I have for you,' declares the Lord, 'plans to prosper you and not to harm you, plans to give you hope and a future.' "

She rested in that and came to know in a deeper sense a great promise of the Lord, who had saved her and called her by name: "When you pass through the waters, I will be with you; and when you pass through the rivers, they will not sweep over you. When you walk through the fire, you will not be burned . . . [for] you are precious and honored in my sight, and . . . I love you" (Isaiah 43:2-3).

Diane decided that though she knew all the pat answers, "the more powerless you feel, the more His strength comes through. I was powerless, and He was giving me strength. I faced life differently, with new priorities, new everything."

God prompted His people once again, and they responded. A neighbor told Diane her friends would like to give her a baby shower. A few days later Diane got a call from her Sunday school class to arrange for the time and the date of another shower.

Two baby showers! And for a fourth baby. Diane thought this was unheard of but she glady accepted their offer.

She recalls, "My changing table, stroller, swing, car seat and baby clothes had either been worn out or given away. We needed to start over almost from scratch. All of this communicated to me that one's faith is alive when it is at work helping others. God was using his people to pray and to give as a tangible way of encouraging me. As I opened each gift my hope in God increased because these items were designed for a normal, active infant. My friends believed, and their faith strengthened mine."

During the last month of her pregnancy, Diane began having false labor. She was seeing Dr. Cummings every week and talking to him frequently by phone. He always assured her that the false labor wasn't accomplishing enough to force her to go to the hospital, so there weren't any meaningless trips to the maternity ward. The most important appointment Diane made before the big day in November was with the anesthesiologist, Dr. Davis.* She told

* Not his real name.

him she had endured natural childbirth with Jeff and then had a much better, much easier time with a spinal block for Shelley. In retrospect she decided that her back was not made for natural childbirth, and of course, especially now. Dr. Davis agreed, but he said her surgery had complicated matters. "We can't administer the block where we usually do, between the fourth and fifth vertebrae. We'll have to do it between the second and third."

Diane didn't care where it was done, as long as it was guaranteed. She didn't want anything to bring on muscle spasms, pain, a slipped disc, or anything close to what she had suffered the previous March. She trusted Dr. Davis's judgment. If he was there, she would be fine. It was another detail she was praying about.

She and Larry had been praying about the availability of a birthing room. They were a fairly new concept in Nashville at that time, so only two or three were available at their hospital. And there were a lot of Nashvillians having babies.

They had seen the birthing room. It seemed such a nice environment and would eliminate the switch from labor room to delivery room. The space was roomier and more comfortable for mother and father. Diane really wanted to try it. She hoped it would work out.

During the first several days of November Diane continued to suffer contractions that hurt and felt like labor but which were still not dilating her. She talked to Dr. Cummings frequently, and they agreed to set November 15 as the date for inducing labor. That somewhat relaxed her, but on November 14 her contractions seemed real. They were more intense and more frequent, and when she called Dr. Cummings late in the day, he told her to come in.

Larry and Diane put the kids to bed, made sure the neighbors were on call, and gave Tracie last-minute instructions. "We're going to the hospital," Larry told them, "and when you wake up, that's where we'll be. When we see you again we'll have a new addition to our family."

As they rode to the hospital Diane wondered what that new addition would mean to their family. A pediatrician in their church had told her, "Each time you add to the number of people in a family it changes the dynamics of that unit. The family has to include that extra person, and it always takes adjusting."

What kind of an adjustment would be needed for a new sister or a new brother, a handicapped child, one that was unable to walk or talk or think like a normal child? Larry says, "We had determined that if indeed we had a handicapped child, we wanted to be good parents of that child, the best we could be."

Larry and Diane were excited as a nurse wheeled her to a labor room, where they would wait for a birthing room. Diane was still hopeful that they could use one, wanting every detail to fall into place to help give her more peace of mind. Dr. Davis came in and told them this was the only night that week he was working. "I'm glad I didn't miss this delivery."

Diane knew God wanted him there. She was already dilated to six centimeters, and her contractions were strong and consistent. "I've got the spinal block prepared," he told her, "but I want you to go as long as you can without it. That's the only way we can tell if the birth process is jeopardizing your spine and whether you'll need a C-section. OK?"

Diane looked disappointed and skeptical, in spite of her faith in Dr. Davis.

"I really don't dare block you too soon and find out that the labor is hurting your spine and you can't feel it to tell us about it. Understand?"

She nodded and began her breathing technique with the next contraction. They had been in the labor room less than an hour when a birthing room became available. Could things be more perfect? Diane and Larry looked forward to the extra special closeness they had always enjoyed when adding a child to their family. It wouldn't be long before all their questions would be answered, all their mysteries solved. Their problems might be just beginning for the rest of their lives, but at least they would know something. And soon.

9
The Choice

They had arrived at the hospital at 10:50 P.M. Traffic had been light. No other prospective mothers were in sight. Dr. Davis had been there on his last night on call. He was a loving doctor, and he would actually spend more time with Diane than anyone else. Even though he had given her the bad news that he wanted to see how long she could go without a spinal block, she trusted him. "I'll be brave," she had said.

As Larry and Diane settled into the birthing room, they quietly discussed how so many things already had fallen together perfectly. They still didn't know what kind of a child would come forth that night or early morning, a boy or girl, deformed or whole, mentally competent or with a brain and nervous system ravaged by radiation and medication. Yet, so far, everything had gone exactly as they had hoped, or better.

Diane had utmost trust in Tracie, responsible and updated at home with neighbors at the ready for emergencies. Larry was his usual supportive self, and they were in a roomy environment that lent itself to happiness and optimism. They were prayed for, eager, and bubbling with anticipation. They believed they were ready for anything, and while their prayers were that God would give them a healthy, whole baby, they certainly had not made any judgments about babies who were otherwise. They would take whatever God gave them as from His sovereign hand.

They wanted to enjoy and cherish every moment. Though she didn't think about it consciously or talk about it, Diane had the feeling at the back of her mind that this was likely her last pregnancy, her last delivery, her last natural-born child. "We didn't even bring the Monopoly game to pass the time," she recalls. "We wanted to remember every detail." During a previous hospital stay, they remember with a smile, Larry had beat Diane in a game, and she threw it away!

Now Larry sat in a nice, big easy chair provided just for dads. Diane's bed, which looked like a hotel room bed in the newly decorated surroundings, was equipped to be modified into a birthing apparatus at the proper time. The end of the bed could be removed and stirrups attached. Behind an understated screen was a mini-nursery so that the baby could be checked there and not have to be whisked away before the parents had got acquainted with it.

Close by, but also unobtrusive, was everything a doctor would need for emergencies and life-support. The only reason Diane would be removed from this private suite was for a C-section. She and Larry didn't want that, for more reasons than the pain and trauma. Larry wanted to be at Diane's side for this birth.

When the nurses weren't bustling in and out to check on Diane's progress, Larry often left his overstuffed chair to sit on the edge of the bed with her. "It's hard to emphasize enough," he says, "what a neat time that was. A relaxed, happy, upbeat night we'll never forget."

As Diane's contractions began coming harder and faster, she dilated to almost eight centimeters and then seemed to stall for about an hour, probably due to the weakness of her back. Her spine was doing fine, but she was suffering from the pain. A fetal monitor attached to the baby's head, inside the uterus, fed the baby's vital signs to a machine printout. A nurse named Faith said, "That irregular heartbeat is good news. It shows the baby has a strong nervous system."

"Praise the Lord!" Diane exulted, and Larry grinned. "You know why that's so exciting for us, Faith?" Diane managed between contractions.

Faith smiled and shook her head.

Diane told her as much of the story as she could before another contraction caused her to cry out. "Oh, please, Dr. Davis! Help me! Can't I have the spinal block now?"

"Give it a little while," he said softly. "The longer the better."

Larry told Faith the rest of the story and discovered that she too was a Christian. *If we were making this up,* Larry thought, *it would be too unrealistic!*

Another nurse came in and spoke in hushed tones with Faith. Faith pressed her lips together and shook her head.

"What is it?" Diane said, bracing herself for another contraction.

"A mother down the hall just gave birth to a baby with both male and female organs."

Faith couldn't know what a fiery dart that was to Diane. After everything had been going so smoothly, now she had been pierced by yet another story of a difficult, traumatic, tragic birth. Had everything gone so well to promise her a perfect baby, or had this news been a warning that what she had feared all along was about to come true?

She was dilated to eight centimeters for more than an hour when Dr. Cummings and Dr. Davis consulted and decided she should be put on an intravenous drip to intensify the contractions. Diane was sure she couldn't take that without the block. "Dr. Davis! Please, help me!" she moaned. "I can't take it anymore. I need that block!"

91

"Soon," he said. When Dr. Bradford made one of his visits to the birthing room, Dr. Davis consulted with him and learned that a C-section would be unnecessary. That was great news to Larry and Diane, but another contraction gripped her.

"Please!" she screamed. "Dr. Davis! Have mercy!"

The night wore on. Dr. Davis was in the room, so Dr. Cummings knew she was in good hands. Two o'clock, three, and four dragged by.

"I wouldn't want to be a doctor," Larry says, "but it was fascinating. And because I had scrubbed up, that was all that was necessary. There was no gown or suffocating mask to deal with. I was in street clothes. I was relaxed and enjoying this, though Diane was nearly delirious with pain, pleading for the block and wanting everything to go faster."

Larry told her to push, which angered her. "I don't want to! Why don't *you* push?!"

A few minutes later she had her worst contraction and screamed.

"Now," Dr. Davis said, and she nearly wept with relief. A spinal block injection dosage comes in a large, ugly needle and syringe, but to Diane it looked like a precious gift. The pain of the injection would be minuscule compared to her contractions anyway. Dr. Davis turned her on her side and deftly thrust the needle between the second and third lumbar vertebrae. The effect was almost instantaneous. The intravenous drip accelerated the contractions, the block eliminated the pain, she began to dilate toward ten centimeters, and her breathing and blowing were all that were keeping the baby within her.

Now, where was Dr. Cummings? *These guys have a sixth sense about this stuff,* Larry thought. *He'll wake up from a middle-of-the-night nap just in time to take over.*

Which is just about what happened. Diane was as relaxed as possible because of the spinal. She knew she would enjoy this birth without fear or the kind of intense, incapacitating pain that had dogged her in the past.

"Boy, did we see a change in the lady's personality," Larry says.

Diane says that she simply knew it would be fun from that point on. Her legs, however, had gone numb and sometimes slipped off the bed. It became Larry's job to hold them on the mattress.

When the spinal block had taken full effect, it also slowed the effect of the intravenous drip. Labor stopped. Dr. Cummings was elsewhere, napping. Diane's legs were not up in stirrups yet. To the untrained eye, it might have looked as though Larry was in charge. Watching. Checking. Holding her legs. Monitoring the vital signs that were constantly being printed out.

"I wondered how Dr. Cummings could sleep at a time like that," Diane admits. "Of course, births are old hat to him. They are always unique and monumental to the parents."

For another hour labor was stalled at just over nine centimeters. Diane was exhausted, eager to see it end. Labor finally kicked in again, now full force. Doctor Cummings was still not there, but Larry and Faith stood watching, Larry's hand on Diane's stomach, both saying "Push! Push! Push!"

"You get to the point," Diane says, "where you don't want anybody telling you to do anything, and you'd just as soon kill the closest person standing there."

She shyly recalls that Larry was the first to see the top of the baby's head. "I have friends," he says, "who would faint at being that involved in a birth, and I'm sure there are things in the operating room I wouldn't want to have anything to do with. But this was a beautiful experience."

OK, doctor, Larry thought, *it's time to come in! Where are you?* He turned to Faith. "Why isn't he here?"

"He knows," she said calmly. "Don't worry. He knows."

For another half hour, as the clock slipped past six in the morning, Larry kept an eye on the top of that baby's head, wanting it to be born and yet praying nothing significant would happen until Dr. Cummings arrived from across the hall. Diane was wary of following Larry's and Faith's commands to push when Dr. Cummings wasn't there yet, but labor was now progressing. The contractions were fast, intense, and regular. The baby seemed to be responding too.

It was time. Diane felt the incredible urge to push. She held her breath and arched her back. Her feet were put into the stirrups. Even with the block she could feel the baby coil itself within her and begin its own push. She huffed and blew, sucked air, held it again, and pushed. And here came Dr. Cummings. Cool. Laid back. In control.

"Good work," he said. "Let's get it done."

Larry had been at Diane's head for the births of Jeff and Shelley. He made room for Dr. Cummings, moving up to be at Diane's side. From there he watched the birth with her in a full length mirror. As he quietly encouraged his wife, she groaned, her face flushed, her body focusing its surprising strength and energy on one task.

Dr. Cummings quickly prepared her and closely monitored the baby's position as the nurses readied his instruments. Diane's eyes were shut tight, her heart pounding, sweat breaking out on her forehead. She was unaware of pain in her back, thought she felt the pressure throughout her torso. She hoped and prayed the baby's vital signs were good but she couldn't think, couldn't turn her head, couldn't open her eyes for a peek at the read-out.

Time seemed to stand still. Everything was ready. Mother and baby and doctor and father and nurses and anesthesiologist knew there was nothing left to do. The Mayfields had arrived at the end of the journey that had begun in secret, without their knowing it. It had begun with a rare night of intimacy they had shared during a brief respite from Diane's paralyzing pain.

What had been conceived within her during those moments, they knew and believed with all their hearts, was of God. This child had been placed there by the Creator of the universe, by a God with a perfect will, with a perfect timing, with a perfect purpose. Against all odds, to a couple who should never have been able to bear children, He had planted a miracle to bless them, to allow them to be tested, to make them grow, to show His glory.

That fertilized egg had developed and grown and had been knit in secret, bombarded by radiation and drugs from the fourth week through the seventh, when the mysterious, wondrous news had been revealed. Diane carried within her a child only God had known was meant to be.

Their decision, their choice, to carry it to term had been one of dedication, of obedience, of sacrifice, of conviction. The ensuing months had been filled with hope and yet also with terror. Diane never knew from one day to the next what images would be forced past her eyes and ears, what she might see and hear about some pitiful childbirth, the result of a woman's making the same unknowing mistake she had made, or the result of a woman her age carrying a baby to term.

They had prayed every day. They had rested in the God of their forefathers. They had followed their beliefs into the dark, unknown world of faith. And they were ready and willing to accept this child as a gift of God. Regardless. "Just let it live," they prayed silently. "Let it be born alive, and we can deal with anything after that. This is a child on loan to us from You, and we have already pledged to give it back to You."

At exactly six-thirty in the morning on November 15, 1985, Diane Mayfield took one more gigantic swallow of air, pointed her toes, balled her fists, knotted her brow, clenched her teeth, and pushed with all her might.

"Here he comes!" Dr. Cummings said. "Push, Mama!"

"Push, Diane!" Faith said.

"Push," Dr. Davis said.

"Push, Babe," Larry said.

Diane heard none of them. The pain had been blocked, but she could feel that baby coming.

The face appeared.

"Oh, man!" Larry said, his throat thick with emotion.

"Hold just a second, Diane," Dr. Cummings said with authority, and as she relaxed for an instant he turned the baby's shoulder. "Go!" he said.

She pushed again, and the baby slid into view.

The doctor deftly sliced the umbilical cord and applied the clamp.

"What do we have here?" he said.

10
Baby Mayfield

"A boy!" Larry said, and Diane wept.

"Jonathan Brian," she said simply. "Jonathan, God's gracious gift." The middle name was for her brother, now gone ten years.

The doctor quickly wiped off the boy as Larry and Diane frantically scanned his body for problems. He was perfect—head and chest in good proportion, limbs, fingers, and toes in total complement. He looked strong and healthy, and as a warming cap was applied and he was wrapped in a blanket, his cavernous eyes darted around the room.

"I don't know what he could see at that point, if anything," Larry says, "but he sure appeared to be checking us out."

"He was absolutely gorgeous," Diane says. Larry was holding her hand, and they were moved to see not the nurse, not the obstetrician, but Dr. Davis, the anesthesiologist, scoop up the baby and deposit him on Diane's chest. He squeaked and gurgled from the beginning.

Larry glanced up at Dr. Cummings as he continued to work on Diane. She seemed healthy and fine. From what he could see of the baby, he looked perfect. But he knew they weren't out of the woods until Jonathan could be examined thoroughly.

Dr. Davis let Diane hold him for a minute, then took him to a tiny basket in the in-room nursery and checked every inch of his body. "This is the most alert newborn I've ever seen," he said.

"I wanted to scream for joy," Diane says. "Yet we were awestruck and very quiet. This was not a hilarious moment; it was a holy one. We were full of wonder. God did this for us! We thanked the Lord for our Psalm 139 baby."

Before Jonathan was taken to the nursery, Diane was allowed to hold him again while Dr. Cummings did his work. Larry dialed the house, and Diane talked to Tracie. "You have a brother!"

"Ah, great!" Tracie said, and she laughed to hear the baby's noises.

She handed the phone to Jeff who reveled in finally getting a brother. "All right!" he said. "A boy!"

Upon hearing that, little Shelley made a beeline for her room upstairs, wailing. "No! I wanted a sister!" She had wanted a girl as much as Jeff wanted a boy.

"Jeff," Diane said, "let me talk to Tracie while you go get Shelley. Tell her I need to talk to her."

"Boy! Girl! Who cares?" Dr. Cummings said. "This baby's healthy!"

When Shelley came tearfully to the phone, Diane said, "Listen to your baby brother." He squeaked.

"I don't want to have anything to do with a boy," she said. "I wanted a girl."

"But you know what?" Diane pressed. "He needs you to teach him to read. Jeff will teach him sports, but you have to teach him to read."

Shelley was silent.

"And you know what else?"

"What?"

"He wants to see you."

"He does?"

"Daddy's going to pick you up from school at lunch time and you can come and see him, OK?"

"OK."

Later Larry would call Shelley's teacher to tell her what she was going through, but the teacher reported that by the time Shelley got to school she was bragging about her new little brother who wanted to see her and whom she was going to teach to read.

The baby was hustled off to the nursery, and Dr. Cummings finished with Diane. A nurse told her to just rest until a room opened up. *Rest?* Diane thought. *It's been a long night, but that's the last thing I want to do.*

What she wanted to do, she says, was to dance down the halls. "I had been through an exhilarating experience, and I wanted everyone to know. I wanted to run and jump and shout, 'My baby is here and he's healthy and beautiful and normal!' I wanted to open all the windows in the place and tell the world."

But since she was still attached to a tube and couldn't move, she obeyed the nurse and tried to rest. And then her pastor visited again and left her with these verses: "Now to Him who is able to do exceedingly abundantly above all that we ask or think, according to the power that works in us, to Him be glory in the church by Christ Jesus throughout all ages, world without end. Amen" (Ephesians 3:20-21, NKJV*).

Meanwhile, Larry was making the usual phone calls, preparing to round up the kids from school at noon, and keeping in touch with the doctors in the nursery, who were double- and triple-checking Jonathan. Anything they found was to be reported to him and to Diane. No secrets, no pro-

* *New King James Version.*

99

tecting the new mother, nothing hidden. Diane and Larry wanted to know everything and be prepared to deal with it.

As Diane lay there, praying that everything would be OK with Jonathan Brian, the excitement of the birth and the thought of her other children getting to meet the new little one kept her awake. She prayed most of the morning, thanking God for the lessons she had learned, the things she never wanted to forget. She renewed her promise to tell the story far and wide, and she listed in her mind the wonderful truths that had been imparted to her over the last several months:

This was God's perfect plan for us, from beginning to end.

The value of intercessory prayer cannot be measured.

Personal experience should be shared freely to encourage others.

God's people are precious when they join to meet the physical needs of those who are hurting.

When pastors and lay people visit the sick at home and in the hospital, they have a ministry of immeasurable effectiveness.

God loves us and shows His goodness in the little details He weaves into our lives.

God is at work creatively, compassionately, and sovereignly, working His will in us as we submit to Him.

The life of the unborn is precious and sacred and inviolate. No human should play God and try to determine its value.

What Diane didn't know was that her pediatrician, Dr. Ellis,* had taken Jonathan to the nursery to check on a potential heart murmur. He had already reported to Larry that everything was fine, from that standpoint.

* Not his real name.

Neighbors visited, and then both the children's pastor and the youth pastor from the church stopped in to say they had just seen Jonathan in the nursery and that he looked beautiful. "Another affirmation," Diane says.

By the time Diane was moved to a regular room, it was time to see the baby again and for Larry to bring the kids in. It was a joyous reunion. Tracie was delighted. Jeff was crazy about his new little brother. And as soon as Jonathan was gently put into her arms, Shelley fell in love with him. Forget her hopes for a little sister. Jonathan became "my baby," then and forever.

Presently the report came from the pediatrician, the obstetrician, and the hospital staff. Jonathan Brian Mayfield was perfect in every way they knew to test.

Ten days later, during Thanksgiving week, Diane and Larry took Jonathan to Arkansas to see his grandparents and meet the many who had prayed for him. They got to see the answer to their prayers, and the Mayfields got a chance to thank them.

A month later Jonathan made his debut on the stage at church as the baby Jesus. The church was packed with weeping people, and though his name was never mentioned, he received a standing ovation. The day after Christmas, Larry and Diane took the baby to Zion, Illinois, to celebrate with Larry's parents.

Less than a month later Jonathan was dedicated. Larry and Diane did not realize when they scheduled it that the Sunday it fell upon was Sanctity of Human Life Sunday. The pastor broke protocol at their request and sang "Children of the Heavenly Father" before praying for the baby and the parents.

During the dedication service, Diane thought, *What could be more fitting than for us to stand before these people who faithfully prayed Jonathan into the world as others marched on the Capitol steps against abortion, which could have taken his life too if we hadn't been obedient to God?*

As Jonathan cried, Pastor Reed began with a light-hearted paraphrase of a New Testament scene: "Then were brought unto Him little children, that He might put His hands on them and pray, and the disciples rebuked them because they cried.

"But Jesus said, 'Don't worry if they cry. Forbid them not to come unto Me, for of such is the kingdom of heaven.'

"In presenting your child for dedication, you not only signify your faith, but also your desire that he may early know and follow the will of God. . . .

"It will be your duty to teach him early the fear of the Lord, to watch over his education that he be not led astray, to direct his youthful mind to the Scriptures, his feet to the sanctuary, and to restrain him from evil associates and habits, and, as much as in you lies, to bring him up in the nurture and admonition of the Lord.

"Are you ready to give him up?"

Diane and Larry, emotion filled, whispered, "Yes."

"Bless your hearts," the pastor said, taking the baby. "And bless *his* heart. Let's join together in prayer. O God, our Heavenly Father, we do here and now dedicate Jonathan Brian Mayfield to Thee. . . . Thank you for him. Thank you for a mom and daddy who loved him before he was born and prayed for him before he was born and who receive him as a gift from you. And for a brother and sisters who love and care. O God, enable this family to surround him with an atmosphere of love and adoration, and may the praise of Your name be on his lips before he knows even what he's saying. Bless this family, enrich them with skills and grace to be the influences they need to be in this little life."

After the prayer, the pastor told the congregation, "The doctor said, 'You are pregnant, but we'd better abort it, because it will not be normal.' Larry and Diane made the decision, normal or not, to keep their baby, and here he is. And he's all perfect. We're so grateful. We place him right back in your hands, as the heavenly Father did, Diane, and may the Lord watch over you and bless you."

As they stood there, Larry and Diane recognized afresh that Jonathan had been given to them only for a while. "He is on loan to us," Diane says, "as are our other children. God has entrusted us to bring them up in His ways, to guide and love him, showing him that only in Jesus will his life have true significance.

"Whenever Larry and I look at our son, we have a clear reminder to praise and glorify God. This is our testimony of His faithfulness. We want people to look at the difficulties they're going through and be able to say, 'He's going to work in my life; He's going to work it out.'

"That's what we want Jonathan's story to be: a ministry to people."

On him have we set our hope
that He will continue to deliver us.
2 Corinthians 1:10

Moody Press, a ministry of the Moody Bible Institute, is designed for education, evangelization, and edification. If we may assist you in knowing more about Christ and the Christian life, please write us without obligation: Moody Press, c/o MLM, Chicago, Illinois 60610.